KERNEL LESSONS

Patrai H. Neill

KERNEL LESSONS INTERMEDIATE

STUDENTS' BOOK

ROBERT O'NEILL
ROY KINGSBURY
TONY YEADON

EUROCENTRE

LONGMAN

LONGMAN GROUP LIMITED
London
*Associated companies, branches and
representatives throughout the world.*

© Eurozentren 1971

First published 1971
Nineteenth impression 1978

ISBN 0 582 52240 4

Printed in Singapore by
Singapore Offset Printing Pte Ltd

Eurocentre Research and Development Unit, Bournemouth.

Illustrated by James Val

ACKNOWLEDGEMENTS

Many people helped the authors at various times while this book was being written and it would be impossible to mention all of them. We wish, however, to give particular mention to:

Miss Jean McNiff, who did the original artwork for the first pilot editions and whose time, attention and criticism later was invaluable in producing the final version.

Miss D. King and Miss J. Croad, who did all the demanding typing involved in the pilot editions and in the final version.

The staffs of the Bournemouth Eurocentre, and the London Eurocentre, who gave a great deal of constructive criticism and comment based on their experience of using the material.

*Robert O'Neill, Roy Kingsbury, Tony Yeadon.
June 1970.*

Contents

Contents

Foreword

This book represents a further step in our efforts to provide the language-teacher with modern techniques and materials in areas not yet fully covered. Our first four publications were concerned with teaching method and were intended for the teacher. The fifth, *English in Situations,* was course material for the use of both teacher and student.

Kernel Lessons Intermediate is a new development in that it makes a clear-cut division between teacher and student material and contains a full programme of separate materials for the student. This programme, specially designed for the 'faux débutant' or post-elementary student, consists of written material (exercises and informational texts), pictures and tapes.

In the introduction to the Teacher's Book a description is given of how this material can be put to the best use. Both the techniques here described and the course-material itself were continuously utilised and revised in the English Eurocentres for over 2 years before publication.

We believe that with this book we are meeting a real need and that through it teachers and students at this particular level will find more interest and satisfaction in language-teaching and learning.

Erh. J. C. Waespi
Director of the Foundation for European Language and Educational Centres.

The Eurocentres are a group of language schools directed by the Foundation for European Language and Educational Centres, Zürich. The schools offer full-time courses for adult students all the year round, and each language is taught in the country where it is spoken.

Introduction *To the Student*

Who is this book for?

This book has been specially written for Intermediate Students.

These are the special problems:

(i) You perhaps feel that you are no longer making very much progress. Somehow, it seems you are not learning as much as you did when you were a beginner.

(ii) Perhaps you realise that you need practice in some of the fundamentals of English. However, the type of practice you need is not the type of practice beginners need in these fundamentals.

(iii) There is a lot you have already studied but which you have not yet learned. In other words, there are many things which you can understand and have even practised, but which you still cannot use correctly, quickly, and as automatically as a native English-speaker does.

What exactly are the problems?

Problem (i) is probably the most important from the students' point of view. For teachers, problems (ii) and (iii) are the most important. These last two are really almost the same. Let us study each problem.

(i) The feeling that you are making little or no progress.

This is very common. It is partly true and partly an illusion. It is true because after you have passed the beginner's stage in anything, languages, mathematics, science, etc., you always reach a point where it is impossible to learn as much as you did before. This is because things are now more complicated, or seem to be.

It is partly an illusion because a great deal of the progress you make after the beginner's stage is not clear. At the beginner's stage, when you first learn a new thing, you can go away and say 'Today I learned this.' But, of course, you did not really learn it. You only saw it for the first time. But did you learn to use it automatically? Did you learn to use it without thinking about it? As an intermediate student you can make a great deal of progress in this direction: you can learn to use automatically many of the things you saw for the first time when you were a beginner. In many ways, it is the most important type of progress.

(ii) The need to practise certain fundamentals again but not in the same way as beginners do.

You already have a reasonable vocabulary. You have difficulty in using this vocabulary but not too much difficulty in understanding it. You need some more practice in the same things beginners need practice in, but you do not need the same type of practice. You can now practise constructions with a larger vocabulary and in a great variety of situations. This book will sometimes give you practice in some of the things beginners practise, but it will not be the same type of practice.

Remember always that all students, even the most advanced, need this practice. There are certain basic things in English that cannot be mastered without a great deal of practice. You must have this practice over a long period.

(iii) The need to learn some of the things you have already studied.

Learning a language is, in some ways, like learning how to fly or play the piano. There are important differences, but there is a very important similarity. It is this: learning how to do such things needs lots of practice. It is never enough simply to 'know' something. You must be able to 'do' things with what you know. For example, it is not enough simply to read a book on how to fly an aeroplane. A book can give you lots of information about how to fly, but if you only read a book and then try to fly without a great deal of practice first, you will crash and kill yourself. The same is true of playing the piano. Do you think it is enough simply to read a book about it? Can you play the piano without having lots of practice first?

Many language-students think it is enough simply to 'know' a grammar rule or the meaning of a word. They do not understand that there is a difference between such things and the actual capacity to make correct sentences and to use words correctly. You cannot say you know something unless you can

(a) understand it when it is spoken quickly, at normal speed

(b) use and understand it without asking yourself first what it means in your own language

(c) use it quickly and without pausing to think about it.

You must practise speaking and hearing English a great deal before you can have a good command of it. In this course, you will often have to practise things you already understand. Never think it is enough simply to understand something. There are many things you already 'know' which you cannot really use. In this course you will learn to use many of the things you already 'know'.

What must students realise in order to learn more?
The world is full of ex-students of English who stopped at the point you are now at. They stopped learning because they did not realise there is a difference between 'knowing' English and being able to use it. They lost interest because they think they cannot learn. 'I know that but I always make mistakes when I try to use it. I must be stupid!' they say. They are not stupid. They can learn English. What they need is more practice in interesting situations. They need more practice in listening to and using English.

In some ways, the point you are at now in learning English is more important than the beginner's stage. You must go on learning from here, or what you have already learned will be wasted. This course is for such students. You will, then, learn two types of things.

(a) Things which you perhaps have seen before but which you have not really learned to use.
(b) Entirely new things. Things which you have never seen before.

How will you use this book?
The book has 25 Units. It will probably take you between 2 and 3 lessons for each unit. Some groups will take more. A few will take less. Each unit has 6 pages, and these are divided into 5 parts.
PART A (2 pages) The pictures on the left help explain the texts or 'situations' on the right hand page. The situations are typical examples of when we use the new construction you are studying.
In class, first cover the 'situations' and look only at the pictures. Remember these things:
1. Individual words are not so important. Whole situations are very important. Try to understand whole situations even if you do not understand individual words.

2. You can learn to write words later. First learn to use and to pronounce words correctly.
3. Take an active part in the intensive question and answer work here. Do not be afraid to make mistakes. Everybody makes mistakes.
4. After you have done question and answer work with the teacher, use the words next to the picture to ask someone else, perhaps the student next to you, questions about the situation.
5. After this, you can read the situations quietly for a minute in class. Now you can ask any questions you have about words, etc.
PART B (1 page) This is the 'Formation and Manipulation' page. It directs your attention to important facts about the pronunciation and formation (or construction) of what you have done. There is a lot of opportunity here, too, for oral practice in class and written practice at home.
PART C (1 page) This is a simple detective story. It is not very serious but it is very useful. Each Unit has one part or 'episode' of this story. It goes on to the end of the book. In it, you can learn a lot of new words. You can get practice in reading and then talking about it. Sometimes there are examples of things you will learn in the next Unit, too. You can read this at home or quickly in class.
PART D (1 page) We call this 'Further Practice'. It has different special exercises and always a conversation. The conversation teaches you things we say in everyday life, and special things like the words you use when someone apologises to you, or how to say 'pardon' politely. You can listen to these conversations on tape. After you have listened to the tape or to the teacher, you can take parts yourself.
PART E This has a summary (or short version of what you have just learned) and special exercises for homework. The exercises are not the only homework you can do. They are only the minimum. There is also a 'Guided Composition'. This helps you to write a composition about something you have just learned. The compositions become 'freer' or 'less controlled' as you go along. There is also always a 'transfer exercise'. This is more help in using what you have learned in your own examples.

Unit 1
a

Present simple and position of time adverbs

1

(a) Where/Julia?
(b) When/begin?
(c) the manager?

2

(a) Where/work?
(b) start every morning?
(c) get there?
(d) time now?
(e) his wife/always/ to work?

3

(a) What/Tom want?
(b) father's question?
(c) Tom's answer?

4

(a) What/do?
(b) What kind of man?
(c) often watch?
(d) children and dogs?

5

(a) What/do?
(b) house?
(c) car?
(d) How much money?
(e) Who/girl?

6

(a) life?
(b) When/up?
(c) always/ breakfast in bed?
(d) maid's question?
(e) answer?

He/She	never				at 12	Unit **1**
They	often	DOES	(something)		on Thursday	
etc.	always	DO				**a**

1

Julia Frost works in a large office. Work starts at 9 but she often gets there late. She is five minutes late today. It is 5 past 9 (9.05). Two typists are talking about her.

"Does the manager know she often comes late?"

"No, he doesn't. He often comes late too!"

1. Ask where Julia works!
2. What does she often do?
3. Why doesn't the manager know she often comes late?

2

Frank Martin does not work in an office. He works in a factory and he never comes late. Work starts at 7 but he always gets there early. He is five minutes early today. It is 5 to 7 (6.55). His wife always drives him to work.

1. Make sentences about Frank with these words:
   a) in an office   b) factory
   c) late   d) early
2. Ask when work starts!
3. What does his wife always do?

3

Tom Atkins wants to marry Frank's daughter, Susan.

"What do you do?" Frank wants to know.

"I'm a teacher. I teach languages."

"Do you really love my daughter?"

"Yes, I do. I love her and she loves me. We want to get married!"

1. What is Frank's first question and what is Tom's answer?
2. Make sentences about Tom
   a) a teacher   b) languages
3. Make sentences about Tom and Susan.
4. Ask what they want to do!

4

Charles Kay is a famous actor. He acts in horror films like "Frankenstein's Brother." He never watches horror films. He does not like them. He is really a kind man. He likes children and animals and they like him. He lives in a small house in the country.

1. Ask what Charles does!
2. Make sentences about him
   a) in horror films   b) watches
   c) doesn't like   d) a kind man
   e) children and animals f) house

5

Arthur and Deborah Tigers do not live in a small house. They live in a very large one. Arthur is a businessman. He earns a lot of money. His wife is very young. They are very happy.

1. Ask *questions* with these words:
   a) a small house?
   b) Arthur/an actor?
   c) a lot of money?
   d) wife/very old?
   e) happy?

6

Deborah leads a very easy life. She never gets up before 9 and always has breakfast in bed.

"Do you want your breakfast now?" her maid wants to know.

"Yes, please," is Deborah's answer.

1. Ask questions:
   a) a very hard life?
   b) when/up?
   c) where/breakfast?
2. What is her maid's question and what is her answer?

---

1 a) Notice the *s*

He She	work live earn	*s*	in a factory in a large house a lot of money

Make sentences about your father, mother or teacher.

b) Notice how the question is formed

Does	he she	work in a factory live in a large house earn a lot of money	?

Ask someone else questions about his or her father, mother, etc.

---

2 a) Notice there is no *s* with *I, You, We,* and *They*

I You We They	work here live in London earn £30 a week

Make sentences about yourself, the people in the class, etc.

b) Notice how the question is formed

Do	you I they we	work here live there earn a lot	?

Turn the sentences you made in 2a) into questions.

---

3 Notice how *negative* sentences are formed

Julia Tom	does*n't* (does not)	work in a factory
You I We They	do*n't* (do not)	live in that house get to work before 6 earn £5,000 a year

Make true sentences about yourself and other people with *doesn't/don't*

---

4 a) Notice the position of *often, always* and *never*

1	2	3
She We	*never* *often* *always*	comes late come early

What are some of the things you often do?
Also make sentences with *never* and *always*.

b) Notice how the *first word* of a question is always repeated in the answer

Question	Answer
Do you live here?	Yes, I *do*/ No, I *don't*
Does he know?	Yes, he *does*/ No, he *doesn't*
Is he a teacher?	Yes, he *is*/ No, he *isn't*

Think of questions to ask the person next to you. Tell that person to give you a *short* answer.

4

THE MAN WHO ESCAPED

Episode 1

1 Edward Coke used to be an army officer, but he is in prison now. Every
day is exactly the same for him.

It is winter now and Coke and all the other men get up at six, when it
is still cold and dark. They have breakfast at six thirty. Work begins at
seven thirty. Some of the men work in the prison factory, where they   5
make mail-bags, but Coke often works in the fields outside.

2 The men have lunch at twelve. Lunch lasts an hour and then the men
go back to work again. Dinner is at six. Coke usually goes to the prison
library after dinner and reads until 9.30. The lights go out at ten.

The day is long, hard, and boring and every man has a lot of time to   10
think. They usually think about why they are there. Coke does. He
always thinks about two men.

3 One of the men is called Eric Masters. He used to be an army officer,
just like Coke. Coke knows that Masters has a lot of money now. The
second man's name is Hugo. That is all Coke knows about him. Masters   15
knows where and who Hugo is, but Coke doesn't.

Every night Coke lies in bed and thinks about Eric Masters and Hugo.
There is another thing he thinks about, too. Escaping. He wants to
escape and find Masters, and then the other man. Coke is in prison for
something he did not do.   20

FURTHER PRACTICE

1. Invention Exercise

MODEL:

He She	often never always	does that

PROMPT: football on Saturdays

RESPONSE: He always plays football on
Saturdays

or: He never watches football on
Saturdays

Prompts:

a) the theatre at week-ends
b) jazz
c) tea without sugar
d) to work by bus
e) French magazines
f) to the seaside in winter
g) brown bread
h) detective stories
i) coffee with cream
j) Turkish cigarettes

2. Conversation

Tom Atkins teaches languages at a Technical
College. It is the teabreak. He is in the staff-
room. There is another teacher there, too. His
name is Ken Grimes, a friend of Tom's. Tom
is smoking.

KEN: (sniffing) Phew! Is that a French cigarette?

TOM: Pardon?

KEN: Is that a French cigarette you're smoking?

TOM: Yes, that's right. Why? What's the matter?

KEN: I don't understand how you can smoke
French cigarettes. They make a terrible
smell.

TOM: I like them very much. I prefer them to
English cigarettes.

KEN: Have you got a lot of them?

TOM: Yes, about 200, why?

KEN: Well . . . er . . . could I buy some from
you?

TOM: Buy some from me? But . . . you don't
like French cigarettes!

KEN: No, I don't. But my wife does. I can't
understand it.

Questions

1. What does Tom say when he doesn't
understand Ken's question?
2. Why doesn't Ken like French cigarettes?
3. What does Ken want to do when he hears
Tom has 200 French cigarettes?
4. Ask and answer why he wants to do this!

Practice

1. Repeat after the teacher or tape recorder
Tom's intonation of 'Pardon!'
2. Make some sentences of your own with
"Could I . . . . ?"
3. Observe the word order

    1   2   3

"I like them very much"

Think of some things you like very much.
Use the same word order.

e   Summary

Focal points in this Unit

1. Sentences like "He works in a factory", "She often comes late" and "They live in a large house" are all in the *Present Simple Tense*.

   Notice that in the situations the tense does *not* tell you what the people are doing at the moment. For instance, in situation 2, Tom says, "I teach foreign languages". That is *not* what he is doing at the moment.

   One of the main uses of this tense is to talk about what people often, always, never, or usually do. That is why we must use it when we want to say what Edward Coke does every day.

2. Remember that 'always', 'often', 'never', and 'usually' (Adverbs of Frequency) always go in front of the main verb.

       1   2   3

   "He always does that!"

3. Remember how we ask questions ("Does he work in a factory?") and how we make negative sentences ("They don't live in a small house"). Look at the Formation and Manipulation page for this.

4. The question "What do you do?" or "What does he do?" is often used to ask what a person's *job* is. It is *never* used to ask about someone's actions at the moment! For this, we use the question, "What is he doing?" and "What are you doing?" (See Unit 2)

f   Exercises for homework

1. Make these sentences into questions and then into negatives like this:—
   Harry works in an office.
   Does Harry work in an office?
   No, Harry doesn't work in an office.
   a) Julia works in a factory.
   b) Arthur and Deborah live in a small house.
   c) Deborah is old.
   d) Arthur and Deborah are poor.
   e) People in prison lead an easy life.
   f) Charles acts in cowboy films.
   g) Tom and Susan want to get married next year.

2. **Guided Composition**
   Read lines 4 to 9 of the Episode again carefully and then, using the same sentence patterns, write about this person:

   Julia/breakfast/8.15//work/9//often late// lunch/12.30//lunch/an hour and a half// work/ finish/5.30//dinner/6.30//usually/ television/after dinner//often read/10.45// never/to bed before 11//

3. **Transfer Exercise**

   Write true sentences (at least 4) about yourself, friends and family. Use the pattern, "I/we . . . never/always . . . ."

Present continuous

1

(a) What time?

(b) What/Deborah?

(c) What/maid?

(d) Where/Frank?

(e) the men/breakfast?

(f) What/talking about?

2

(a) What/Deborah/friends?

(b) they/lunch?

(c) What/one of them/wearing?

(d) Where/Frank?

(e) Frank/always/there?

(f) What/a lot of men?

(g) waiting for?

3

(a) Where/Arthur and Deborah?

(b) What/Deborah?

(c) Why/Arthur/the man?

(d) What/Frank?

(e) What/wife?

(f) What/Susan?

(g) Frank/a film?

4

(a) Who/Susan/to?

(b) Where/Tom/from?

(c) Susan's questions?

(d) What/Frank and his wife?

(e) Susan upstairs?

(f) Where/she?

1

It is half past nine (9.30). Deborah is having breakfast and listening to some music on the radio. The maid is carrying a tray with some more coffee on it.

Frank is in the factory. The men there are not having breakfast. It is their tea-break. They are talking about a football match this evening.

1. Ask questions with these words:
   a) What/Deborah   b) the maid
   c) Where/Frank   d) the men/breakfast
   e) talking about
2. Make some sentences with "isn't" and "aren't" (Frank/the radio, etc.)

2

It is half past eleven. Deborah and her friends are not having lunch. They are having 'morning coffee'. They are talking about their husbands. One of them is wearing a very strange hat.

Frank is eating in the factory canteen. He always eats there. A lot of men are standing in a queue. They are waiting for their lunch. It is raining outside.

1. Ask and answer these questions about Deborah and her friends:
   a) lunch   b) What
   c) football   d) Deborah/a strange hat
2. Ask these questions about Frank and the other men here:
   a) morning coffee   b) Frank/always
3. What are the men behind him doing and what are they waiting for?

3

It is 9 o'clock in the evening. Arthur and Deborah are at the opera. Deborah is whispering something to Arthur and he is looking at the man next to her. The man is disturbing her because he is snoring.

Frank is watching television but his wife and Susan are not. Susan is reading and her mother is writing. Frank is watching a football match.

1. Ask and answer questions about Arthur and Deborah:
   a) a football match   b) Why/whispering
   c) What/looking at   d) Why
2. Ask and answer these questions about Frank and his family:
   a) Susan and her mother/television
   b) Frank/an opera
3. Ask and answer what each person in the picture is doing!

4

It is 11 o'clock. Susan is talking to Tom. He is phoning from Paris. "Are you having a good time? What's the weather like? Is it raining?" she wants to know.

Frank and his wife are getting ready for bed. He can hear Susan downstairs. "Who's she talking to?" he is asking.

1. What is Susan doing and where is Tom phoning from?
2. What are the questions Susan is asking?
3. Ask what Frank is doing and what he is asking!

9

FORMATION AND MANIPULATION

1 Pronunciation

a) Practise the weak form of *is, are* and *am* in these typical examples

    i)   Frank*'s* at the factory. He*'s* working

    ii) They*'re* watching an opera.

    iii) What*'s* she doing?

    iv) Where*'re* you going?

b) Practise the strong form in these simple questions (when *is, are* or *am* begin the questions)

    i)   Am I speaking too fast?

    ii) Is the bus coming?

    iii) Are you waiting for the bus?

2

a) Notice the word after *he, you, I,* etc.

I	*am* ('m)	learning English
He She	*is* ('s)	watching television
You We They	*are* ('re)	listening to the teacher disturbing those people

b) Notice the position of *is, are* and *am* in questions

Am	I	
Is	my radio	*disturbing* you?
Are	we	

Make at least six sentences from 2 a) into questions

c) Notice how the *negative* is formed

I am	
She is	*not* listening
They are	

Pronunciation Note: In speaking, we usually say 'is*n't*' and 'are*n't*'. It is only with *I* that we *must* use *not* in its full form. ('I'm not listening')

Use 2 a) again to make two negative sentences each with *He, You* and *I* (6 sentences in all)

3 Notice the position of words like *to, at* and *for* (prepositions) in these questions with *Who* and *What*.

What		waiting *for*	
	are you	looking *at*	?
Who		listening *to*	

Look at the picture situations again. Start at situation 2 and think of questions like these for the people in the situations.

THE MAN WHO ESCAPED
Episode 2

1   It is six o'clock on a very cold winter evening. All over England people are sitting down in their living-rooms and are watching the news on television or are listening to it on the radio. There is one very important piece of news this evening. It is this.

     "In the West of England this evening, hundreds of policemen are 5
looking for a man who escaped from Princeville Prison early this morning. The man's name is Edward Coke. He is 30 years old, six feet tall, and has black hair and blue eyes. He is wearing a dark blue prison uniform. The police do not think he can stay free very long. It is only a few degrees above zero and it is snowing." 10

2   The radio is on in an expensive pub in Soho, in the centre of London. Most of the people there are not very interested in the news programme, but one man is. His name is Eric Masters. He is about 45 and is wearing very expensive clothes. He is looking very afraid of something. There is another man standing next to him at the bar. Masters is asking him 15
a question.

"Did they say the man's name was Coke?"

"Yes, that's right. Coke . . . Edward Coke. Why? Do you know him?"

"Pardon?"

"Do you know him?" 20

"No . . . no, I don't know him . . . I . . . I just wanted to know the man's name, that's all."

3   In another part of London, a young detective is standing in the office of his chief at Scotland Yard. The young detective's name is Richard Baxter. 25

"You knew Coke, didn't you, Baxter?"

"Yes, sir. I arrested him four years ago."

Baxter's chief is nodding his head.

"Yes, I know that, Baxter. That's why I'm giving you this order, now. Find Coke again! You must find him immediately!" 30

1. Invention Exercise

Make questions using the prompts

Example:

PROMPT: I/too fast?

RESPONSE: Am I driving too fast?

or: Am I speaking too fast?

Prompts:

a) I/your seat?
b) you/a good time?
c) Julia/lunch now?
d) Frank/a football match?
e) we/too much noise?
f) you/the news?
g) those people/about me?
h) that woman/a cigar?
i) Deborah/up?

2. Conversation

A TALKATIVE OLD LADY

(The information office in a railway station. We can hear the sounds of trains coming and going and announcements over the loudspeakers)

OLD LADY: Good afternoon. I'd like some information about the trains, please.

CLERK: Yes, madam. Which train? Where are you going?

OLD LADY: To Bournemouth. You see, I have a sister there and . . .

CLERK: So your question is 'When's the next train to Bournemouth?' Is that right?

OLD LADY: Yes, that's right. When's the next train to Bournemouth, please?

CLERK: At half past four. That's in about a minute.

OLD LADY: Thank you very much. Oh! Can I get something to eat on the train? I always have something to eat when I travel. I find that a cup of tea and a sandwich always help my nerves.

CLERK: Yes, madam. There's a buffet car on the train.

OLD LADY: Oh, good! Er . . . how much does a cup of tea cost?

CLERK: I'm not sure, madam. Eightpence, I think.

OLD LADY: Eightpence! Oh dear! Things are getting so expensive!

CLERK: Yes, madam. Your train's going to leave in half a minute now.

OLD LADY: Thank you. Oh! Which platform does it leave from?

CLERK: Platform 13.

OLD LADY: Platform 13! Oh, dear! I never travel on trains that leave from platform 13! 13's an unlucky number. When's the next train after the 4.30?

Questions

a) Without looking at the text, ask the questions the old lady did, using these words:
   i) next train to Bournemouth ii) platform
   iii) something to eat

b) What does the old lady always do when she travels? Ask why and answer!

c) What is it that she never does? Ask why and answer!

Practice

a) Make questions of your own using these two patterns
   i) When's the next . . . to . . .?
      Prompts:
      bus/town-centre
      plane/London
      ship/Australia
   ii) How much does (or *do*) . . . cost?
      Prompts:
      those cigarettes. a bottle of whisky.
      that camera. those shoes.
      that sweater. a ticket to Manchester.

e   Summary

Focal points in this Unit

1. Sentences like 'Where are you going?', 'Frank is watching television', etc. are in the *Present Continuous Tense.*

   Notice that in the situations in this Unit the tense is used to say what people are doing at the moment, at the time you see them. As soon as you want to talk about what they sometimes, always or usually do, you go back to the Present Simple tense. For instance, in situation 2 on page 9 we say 'Frank *is eating* in the factory canteen. He always *eats* there'.

2. Study the Formation and Manipulation page carefully. Notice how questions and negative sentences are formed. Notice that in the negative, we rarely say *not* in its full form. In speaking, we usually say:

   'He is*n't* coming' and 'They are*n't* watching an opera.'

   It is only with *I* that we must say *not* in its full form.

   'I'm *not* waiting for the bus'.

3. Notice that we usually use the Present Simple tense when we ask when a train leaves, or a bus arrives. (See Conversation, page 12). We do this because we are thinking of what the timetable says.

f   Exercises for homework

1. Do all the questions and other exercises on pages 9 and 10.

2. Notice how these prompts are used to make *two* sentences.
   Deborah/always up/9.30=Deborah always gets up at 9.30. It is 9.30 now and she is getting up.
   Do the same with these prompts (two sentences each):
   a) Frank/breakfast/6.15
   b) Arthur/to work/8 o'clock
   c) Deborah/usually lunch/1.30
   d) Frank/usually/the television news/ 10 o'clock.
   e) I/the radio/6 o'clock

3. Make sentences of your own with these words:
   listen to. talk to. talk about. wait for. look at.
   Example: I'm waiting for a bus. Deborah never listens to the 8 o'clock news.

4. **Guided Composition**

   Read the news item from the Episode again carefully (page 11, lines 5–10) and then, using the same sentence patterns, write another piece of news with these prompts:
   North of Scotland/dozens of detectives/ young woman/a prison late last night// Jane Stone//26/five feet six inches/blonde/ blue//grey dress/black shoes//weather/ terrible/police/free very long//snow/very cold//

5. **Transfer Exercise**

   Write 5 true sentences about things that are happening or about what other people are doing *now* while you are doing this exercise.

Simple past tense
(Regular and irregular verbs)

1

(a) late this
     morning?
(b) eat?
(c) drink?
(d) the dishes?
(e) much time?

2

(a) friend's
     question?
(b) Where/
     manager?
(c) When/he
     Julia?

3

(a) How often
     London?
(b) London
     yesterday?
(c) friend's
     question?
     (on time
     yesterday?)

4

(a) Where/Arthur/
     this morning?
(b) Where/
     Deborah/
     station?
(c) Deborah's
     question?
(d) Who/Arthur/
     meet?
(e) train early?

5

(a) Tom and
     Susan/this
     morning?
(b) What/now?
     (champagne/
     cake/good
     time)
(c) What/Susan's
     father?

6

(a) Who/at the
     party?
(b) What/all do?
(c) Tom's mother?
(d) What/Frank?

1

Julia often gets up late and she got up late this morning. She ate some cornflakes and drank some tea. She did not wash all the dishes. She washed only some of them. She did not have very much time this morning.

1. Is Julia getting up now?
2. Is she eating cornflakes and drinking tea now?
3. Tell me three things she did this morning!
4. What did she do with the dishes and why?

2

Julia is having lunch with a friend. "Were you late again this morning?" her friend wants to know. "Yes, I was, and the manager was in the office, too!"
  "Oh? Did he see you?"
  "Yes, he did. He saw me when I came in."

1. What is Julia doing?
2. What are the exact words of her friend's question and Julia's answer?
3. Ask if the manager saw her!
4. Ask when!

3

Arthur often goes to London. He is going there today and he went there yesterday, too. He is talking to an old friend. "Does this train usually arrive on time?" his friend wants to know. "Yes, it does, but it didn't yesterday. It arrived late!"

1. Ask what Arthur often does!
2. Ask what he is doing now!
3. Ask if he did yesterday!
4. What is his friend's question?
5. What is Arthur's answer?

4

Arthur is back from London. He went there this morning. Deborah is at the station to meet him. "Did you have a good time in London?" she wants to know. "Yes, I did, and I met an old friend on the train this morning."
  "Did the train get into London on time?"
  "No, it didn't. It was late again!"

1. Ask and answer questions about Arthur:
   a) When/London   b) a good time
   c) When/old friend d) Where
   e) train on time

5

Tom and Susan got married this morning. They are having a party now. Susan's parents are there and so are Tom's. They are drinking champagne, eating cake and having a good time. Only Tom's mother is unhappy. Susan's father is making a speech.

1. What did Tom and Susan do this morning?
2. Ask what they are doing now!
3. Ask questions with   a) eat   b) drink
4. Ask these questions:
   a) good time   b) Tom's mother
5. What is Frank (Susan's father) doing?

6

Tom and Susan had a party here this afternoon. Tom's parents were there and so were Susan's. Everybody ate cake, drank champagne and had a good time. Only Tom's mother did not eat or drink very much. She was unhappy. Frank made a speech.

1. Ask and answer questions with these words:
   a) When/a party   b) Tom's parents there
   c) Susan's too   d) What/drink and eat
   e) a good time   f) Tom's mother happy
   g) eat very much   h) Frank/speech

1 a) Notice what happens to *regular* verbs in the past

> The train usually arri*ves* on time
>   It arriv*ed* late yesterday
> We usually arriv*e* on time
>   We arriv*ed* late yesterday

b) Notice how the question and the short answer are formed

> Did it arrive on time yesterday?
> No, it *didn't* (or 'Yes, it *did*')
> Did you arrive on time yesterday?
> Yes, I *did* (or 'No, I *didn't*')

Now do this yourself. Make 3 sentences for each of these, like this:

Julia usually washes the dishes=SHE WASHED THEM YESTERDAY
                              DID SHE WASH THEM YESTERDAY?
                        SHE DIDN'T WASH THEM YESTERDAY

i) The train usually arrives on time.
ii) We often arrive late.
iii) Work usually starts at 9.
iv) Frank usually watches television.

v) You usually listen to the news.
vi) Susan and Tom often talk about money.
vii) Arthur often works late.
viii) He usually phones her.

2 a) Notice what happens to *irregular* verbs in the past

> Arthur often *goes* to London
>   He *went* there yesterday
> We often *go* to the opera
>   We *went* there last week

b) Notice that we form the question and the negative *exactly* as we do with regular verbs

>   He *went*
> *Did* he *go*?   He did*n't* go

Now do this yourself, like this: He went to London=WHEN DID HE GO TO LONDON?

i) Julia got to work.
ii) Tom and Susan got married.
iii) We had a party.

iv) They drank all the champagne.
v) I ate all the cake.
vi) Frank made a speech.

3 Notice which people we use *was* with and which people we use *were* with. Also notice the question form and the short answers

I He She It	*was*	late here in London early	yesterday last week last month
You We They	*were*		

Question: Was the train late yesterday?
Answer: Yes, it was (or 'No, it wasn't')

Make sentences from this table with all the various persons.
Then ask the person next to you questions with 'Were you . . .?'
Tell that person to give a short answer!

THE MAN WHO ESCAPED
Episode 3

1 It is 6.30 in the evening now, and the wind is still blowing. It is getting
   colder. About ten miles away from Princeville Prison a man is hiding
   in a field. The wind is cutting through his thin prison uniform like a
   knife.

   A dog is barking somewhere in the distance. Is it a police dog perhaps?   5
   The man in the field does not know. There is only one idea in his mind
   at the moment: he must find food and some warm clothes, but where?

2 Two hundred miles away in London, Baxter's train is standing at platform 9 in Paddington Station. Baxter is sitting in a comfortable compartment. There is another man opposite him. Baxter does not know   10
   the man but he can see he wants to talk. The man is holding a newspaper
   in his hands.

   "I see someone escaped from Princeville Prison this morning."

   "Oh, really?"

   "Yes . . . Would you like to read about it? It's all here in the paper."   15

   "No, thank you."

3 The train is leaving the station now. Baxter is looking out of the window.
   He can see a thousand bright lights in the windows of pubs, cafés,
   houses and flats. Everywhere people are sitting down to warm meals and
   hot cups of tea. The world looks warm and comfortable.   20

   The man opposite Baxter is still talking.

   "The paper says the man was a spy . . . he gave important military
     secrets away. I hope the police catch him!"

   "Yes, so do I."

1. Invention Exercise

1) Use the prompts to make sentences:
   Example:
   PROMPT: to London last Thursday
   RESPONSE: I went to London last Thursday.
        or: We drove to London last Thursday.

   Prompts:

   a) late yesterday morning
   b) fish for breakfast yesterday
   c) television yesterday evening
   d) out for a walk last Saturday
   e) a good time at the party last night
   f) the news on the radio yesterday
   g) a good film last night
   h) football last Wednesday afternoon
   i) married in 1962
   j) 3 bottles of champagne last night

2) Now use the same prompts as in (1) to make negative sentences:
   Example:
   PROMPT: to London last Thursday
   RESPONSE: I didn't go to London last Thursday.
        or: They didn't drive to London last Thursday.

3) Now ask questions using the same prompts as in (1):
   Example:
   PROMPT: to London last Thursday
   RESPONSE: Did you go to London last Thursday?
        or: Did he drive to London last Thursday?

2. Conversation

Tom and Susan are in Tom's sports car. They are at a petrol station.

TOM: Three gallons of super, please.
ATTENDANT: Three gallons of super; yes, sir.
SUSAN: Tom . . . why don't we get a small family car?
TOM: What? You mean, sell my sports car? Never!
SUSAN: But it's expensive to run and it's old. You bought it long before I met you. When did you get it?

TOM: It's a very good car, and I never have any trouble with it!
SUSAN: But you had some trouble with it only last week. Don't you . . .?
ATTENDANT: Er . . . excuse me. That's £1, sir.
TOM: Here you are. Oh, and would you check the battery, please?
ATTENDANT: Check the battery, sir? Certainly.
SUSAN: Don't you remember? It broke down just before we got married and it was in the garage for a whole week!
TOM: This is a wonderful car! It always starts first time!
ATTENDANT: The battery's all right, sir.
TOM: Thank you.
SUSAN: It didn't start first time yesterday morning!
TOM: That was only because it was so cold! It's a wonderful engine. Just listen to it when I start it now! (Presses starter. Sound of engine turning over but not starting.)
SUSAN: I'm listening, Tom.

Questions

1. How does Tom ask the attendant for petrol and to check the battery?
2. When did Tom buy the car and what does Susan say about it?
3. What happened the week before they got married?
4. What happened yesterday morning? What explanation does Tom give?

e   Summary

Focal points in this Unit

1. *Ate, drank, washed, arrived,* etc. are all verbs in the *Simple Past Tense.*

2. We use the Simple Past tense with Adverbs of Past Time, like 'yesterday', 'last week', 'last Friday' etc.

3. Sometimes we do not actually put these Adverbs of Past Time in the sentence. They are only in our minds. We still use the Simple Past tense.

4. There are two main types of verb.
   a) *Regular verbs:* 'wash*ed*', 'watch*ed*' 'play*ed*'
   b) *Irregular verbs:* 'see/*saw*', 'get/*got*', 'go/*went*' etc.

5. We use the same system to form questions and negatives in the past as we do in the simple present. In other words, the past form of 'Do/Does', which is 'Did', is used with the base form of the verb:
   Examples: 'He went there'–'He did not *go* there.' 'Did he *go* there?'

6. *Was* and *Were,* of course, do *not* use this system. Just like *Am/Is/Are,* questions are formed through *inversion,* and the negative with *not.*
   Examples: 'Was he here yesterday?' 'He was not here yesterday.' 'Were you here last week?' 'We were not here last week.'

7. In speaking, we usually use the weak form of *not.*
   Examples: 'He did*n't* come.' 'He was*n't* here.'

f   Exercises for homework

1. Do all the questions and exercises on pages 15 and 16.

2. Make questions with 'What/Where/When did you/they etc. do . . .?' to which the following prompts are possible short answers.
   Example:

   PROMPT: On the train
   You write: Where did you meet him?
   or: Where did you see her?
   or: Where did he read that newspaper article?

   Prompts:

   a) Last Saturday   f) Cornflakes
   b) About 11.30   g) In September 1965
   c) To the opera   h) A new hat
   d) At the station   i) Last summer
   e) In London   j) Champagne, of course

3. **Guided Composition**

   Read situations 1 and 3 (page 15) carefully again, and then write about this person, using the prompts:
   Charles Brown/often/Paris//there today/ last Monday too//late this morning//only time/coffee//train to London/late too// now/10 o'clock plane//usually/9 o'clock//

4. **Transfer Exercise**

   Write 5 true sentences about things you did, people you met or places you went to yesterday.

Unit 4

a

Mass and unit

1

200
£30·40 a week
40 hours a week

(a) Arthur/shop?
(b) newspaper man's questions? (men?/money?/hours?)

2

1948
£7 a week
48 hours
£4 a week
44 hours

(a) When/in a factory?
(b) 36 hours?
(c) How much/earn?
(d) Where/Joan?
(e) she/48 hours?
(f) she/£10?

3

1950

(a) What/1950?
(b) Why/job?
(c) Why/Arthur/better job?

4

1951
£70 a month
44 hours a week

(a) When/Arthur/better job?
(b) hours?
(c) earn?
(d) What/buy?

5

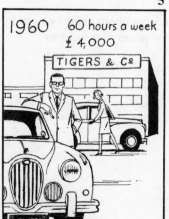

1960
60 hours a week
£4,000
TIGERS & Cº

(a) own factory?
(b) How many hours?
(c) money?
(d) life easier?
(e) cigars?
(f) small car?
(g) wife/car?

6

1963
1968

(a) What/1963?
(b) Who/come?
(c) Who/children?
(d) When/Arthur/Deborah?
(e) When/they/married?

1

Arthur owns a factory. A newspaper man wants to write an article about it.

"How many men work for you?"

"About 200"

"How much do they earn?"

"£30 to £40 a week"

"How many hours do they work?"

"40 hours a week"

1. Why is the newspaper man asking these questions?
2. Ask the same questions:
   a) men   b) earn   c) hours

2

Before Arthur started his own factory he worked in one. He started in 1948. He worked 48 hours a week or more. He never earned more than £7 a week. He had another wife then. Her name was Joan and she sold underwear in a department store. She worked 44 hours a week and earned £4. Life was not easy.

1. What did Arthur do before he started his own factory?
2. What did his wife do?
3. Ask these questions about them both:
   a) hours a week   b) earn

3

Joan had to give up her job in 1950, when she had a baby. She did not want to, but she had to. She often said "You have to find a better job, Arthur. You simply have to!"

Arthur had to find a better job because they did not have enough money.

1. What did Joan have to do in 1950?
2. Ask why!
3. What did she often say?
4. Why did Arthur have to do this?

4

Arthur came home one day in 1951 and said "I found a better job today" "Oh? How many hours do you have to work? How much do you earn?" Joan asked. "£70 a month for 44 hours a week" he said. Joan had another baby that year and he bought a house.

1. Ask and answer questions with "When . . .?"
   a) home and say "a better job"
   b) another baby
   c) a house
2. Ask questions with "How much" or "How many"
   a) hours a week
   b) money a month
   c) children at the end of the year

5

Arthur started his own factory in 1960. He had to work 60 hours a week at first but he earned £4,000 that year. Life was not easier but it was better. He smoked 5 or 10 cigars a day and drove a large car. His wife had a car, too.

1. What happened in 1960?
2. How many hours a week did he have to work at first?
3. Ask questions with a) cars   b) cigars

6

His first wife died in 1963. His children were young and his sister had to come and live with them. She had to look after the children. He met Deborah in 1968 and married her the same year. Deborah is his second wife.

1. What happened in 1963?
2. What did his sister have to do?
3. Ask why!
4. What happened in 1968?
5. Is Deborah his first wife?

1 Notice the words that go with 'How *much*' and those that go with 'How *many*'

a)

How *much*	time money petrol beer wine	have you got?

b)

How *many*	cigarettes hours bottles of beer glasses of wine	did he have?

Which of these words do you think go with 'How much' and which with 'How many'? Make questions with '. . . have you got?/do you want?'

i) chocolate
ii) pieces of chocolate
iii) bread
iv) sandwiches
v) eggs

vi) bacon
vii) steak
viii) pieces of steak
ix) champagne
x) wine

xi) glasses of beer
xii) children
xiii) petrol
xiv) tobacco
xv) cigars

2 Look at this:

Frank *has*	to get up early every day and $\begin{smallmatrix}he\\I\end{smallmatrix}$ *had* to get up early yesterday
I *have*	

i) Make sentences like this about someone you know and about yourself.
   Example: 'My teacher has to give a lesson every Monday at this time and I have to listen to it. He had to give one yesterday and I had to listen to it.'
ii) How do you ask questions with this form? If you don't remember, look at situation 4. Ask some questions yourself. Use words like 'you', 'your brother', 'our teacher'.
iii) What is the *past form* of questions with 'have to'? Look at situation 5, question 2. Then ask someone else questions like that with:
   get up very early yesterday, do a lot of homework last week, work very hard when you were a boy/girl?, etc.
   Notice that the answers are 'Yes, I *did*' or 'No, I *didn't*'

3 Look at this:

He *found* a better job.	When did he *find* a better job?

Ask the same sort of question with these new irregular verbs, all of which are from the situations.
   sold underwear, *came* home, *bought* a new house, *said* 'I found a better job today'

THE MAN WHO ESCAPED
Episode 4

NOTE: From this point onwards, there is a synopsis at the beginning of every episode. The synopsis tells in a few words what happened in the last episodes.
The story is also told in the *past tense* from now on.

SYNOPSIS: *A young detective, Richard Baxter, arrested Coke four years ago. Coke escaped from prison because he wanted to find two men, Eric Masters and someone called 'Hugo'. That was all Coke knew about the second man. He knew Masters when they were officers in the army. Baxter, the detective, left London on the same day Coke escaped. His job was to catch Coke again.*

1   Baxter got on the train at 5 o'clock. An hour later, at 6, he was asleep in the warm train compartment. Coke was still in his hiding-place in a field, 100 miles away. The winter evening got darker and colder. The wind cut through Coke's thin uniform like a knife. Coke was hungry and tired, and his arms and legs were so cold that he could hardly feel   5
them. He knew he had to find food, warm clothing, and a warm place somewhere. "I have to make a move! I can't just stay in this field and die of the cold!" he thought.

2   Coke got up and began to walk. "Where am I? Which direction am I walking in? Am I going back towards the prison?" he asked himself.   10
A few minutes later, the moon came out and Coke could see better. He stopped and looked around. Suddenly he saw a small light not far away. "What can it be? It can't be a car. It isn't moving! It must be a house!" he said to himself and began to walk towards it. The light got larger. It was a house! He could see the form of the roof in the darkness.   15

3   Ten minutes later he was outside the house. He stopped and listened. "Strange!" he thought. "I can't hear anything, not even a radio or a television, but there must be someone in there! There's a light on!" Just at that moment, a thought struck him.
"This is probably the only house around for miles! The police know   20
I'm probably around here somewhere; and if they're anywhere, they're in that house, waiting for me!"
Coke did not move. The wind became colder. His feet and hands felt like ice in the snow. "I have to take the chance! I have to! This is the only place I can find warm clothes and food!" he thought.   25

23

Unit 4
d

1. Invention Exercise

You are talking to Tom Atkins about his job.
He teaches languages at a Technical College,
remember. Ask him questions with 'How much/
How many . . .?' using the prompts.

Example:

a) PROMPT: students/at the College this year
   RESPONSE: How many students are there at
             the College this year?
b) PROMPT: homework/every evening
   RESPONSE: How much homework do the
             students do every evening?

Prompts:

a) free time/every week
b) teachers/at the College this year
c) lessons/every day
d) students/your class this year
e) work/in the evenings
f) books/in a month

Now use the same prompts again to ask
questions about *last year, yesterday, last week*
etc.

2. Conversation

Tom and Susan bought a house last month.
They have not got very much money and Susan
is adding up all the money they spent on food
and other things last week.

SUSAN: We spent £12 last week. £12! That's
too much!

TOM: Er . . . that reminds me . . . did I tell
you about the party?

SUSAN: Party? What party?

TOM: Well . . . er . . . you see, there's a
tradition at the College. When a teacher there
buys a house he has to . . . he has to . . .

SUSAN: 'has to give a party'? Is that what you're
going to say?

TOM: Yes, I'm afraid so. So we need some
beer and wine and cheese for tomorrow
evening.

SUSAN: What? Tomorrow evening! Why didn't
you tell me this before?

TOM: Well . . . I suppose I forgot. I'm
terribly sorry. I really am!

SUSAN: Oh, well, I suppose if we have to give a
party, we have to. Anyway, we have some
beer already.

TOM: Oh, how much?

SUSAN: At least a dozen bottles. Perhaps more
than that.

TOM: How many? Only a dozen bottles? That
isn't enough.

SUSAN: What do you mean? How many people
did you invite? Only three or four, I hope.

TOM: Er . . . more than that, actually. Now,
don't worry about the money.

SUSAN: What do you mean 'Don't worry about
the money?' Someone has to! You never
worry about it! Now, how many teachers did
you invite?

TOM: Well . . . naturally I had to invite all the
teachers and not just some of them. I *had* to!

SUSAN: All the teachers? But how many teachers
are there at the college?

TOM: Not many, really . . . only 35.

SUSAN: What? 35 teachers! Are you mad, Tom?
It isn't just beer and cheese and wine we
need! We need much more than that! Much
more!

TOM: I don't understand. What do you mean?

SUSAN: We need a bigger house!

Correct these statements

STATEMENT: They spent £10 last week.
RESPONSE: No, they spent £12!

1. They have to give a party because they
   bought a new car.
2. They have to give the party next week.
3. Tom often worries about money.
4. Tom invited only some of the teachers.
5. Susan thinks they need a bigger kitchen.

Now ask and answer the questions:

1. Ask when they have to give the party!
2. Ask why!
3. Ask what they need for the party!
4. Ask questions with 'How much' or 'How
   many':
   a) teachers at the college
   b) bottles of beer and wine tomorrow
   c) cheese

e Summary

Focal points in this Unit

1. 'How *much*' is used with *Mass* words. Typical mass words are *beer, milk, cheese, coffee, money, time.*

2. 'How *many*' is used with *Unit* words. Typical unit words are 'bottles of beer', 'glasses of milk', 'pieces of cheese', 'cups of coffee', 'coins', 'seconds' and 'minutes'.

3. a) 'Have to do' means 'It is necessary to do'.
   b) The past of 'have to' is 'had to'.
   c) Questions are formed with 'Do/does . . . have to . . .?' in the present and 'Did . . . have to . . .?' in the past.
   d) The future is 'Will have to', which is usually pronounced 'I'll have to'.

4. It is not a good thing to try and explain the difference between *have to* and *must* at this point. You need a lot more practice in English first to understand the practical difference. However, notice these points:
   a) *must* has no past and no future form. That is, 'had to' and 'will have to' express the past idea and the future idea.
   b) We usually use *have to* rather than *must* to talk about necessity. A common situation in which we frequently use *must* is when we give someone very strong advice, such as 'You know, you really must save more money!'

f Exercises for homework

1. Answer the questions to the situations on page 21 and do the exercises on page 22.

2. In English, we can say 'How many children have you?', but it is more usual to say 'How many children have you got?', using 'have got' instead of simply *have*. Ask questions with 'How much/How many . . . has he/have you got?' with the prompts.
   Examples:
   a) PROMPT: children/they
      RESPONSE: How many children have they got?
   b) PROMPT: money/he/in the bank
      RESPONSE: How much money has he got in the bank?

   Prompts:
   a) friends/they
   b) cars/they/in that garage
   c) boyfriends/she
   d) cigarettes/you
   e) rooms/you/in your house
   f) brothers/your friend
   g) meat/we/in the fridge
   h) modern furniture/they/in their house
   i) children/your sister
   j) clothes/she

3. **Guided Composition**
   Read again what happened to Arthur from 1948 to 1960 (situations 2, 3, 4 and 5; page 21) then write about this person:

   Jim Brent/teacher/language school/1955// 25 lessons a week/£65 a month//wife/book shop//40 hours/£9 a week//she/give up/1959 /baby//Jim/better job/money//new house/ 1961/wife/another baby//own school/1963// Jim/55 hours/but/£3,500//another new house/new car//wife/new car, too//

4. **Transfer Exercise**
   Write at least 5 true sentences about things you *have to do* today or tomorrow, or about things you *had to do* yesterday or last week.

Some, any, a few, a little

1

(a) demonstrators?

(b) policemen?

(c) soldiers?

(d) tourists?

(e) reporters?

(f) birds interested?

2

(a) What/Susan?

(b) What/want to use?

(c) How much sugar usually/always?

(d) chocolate?

3

(a) When/strike?

(b) Where/policemen and strikers?

(c) What day?

(d) What/most of the men?

(e) reporters there?

4

(a) What/Arthur/order?

(b) waiter bring?

(c) many people?

5

(a) How many men?

(b) any women?

(c) What time?

(d) What/Fred?

(e) What/want?

(f) Fred/any money?

1

This is a small demonstration in a London park. There are some demonstrators and some policemen in the park, but only a few. There are not any soldiers there but there are a few tourists. There are also some reporters there; in fact, there are quite a few. There are also some birds in the trees but they are not very interested in the demonstration.

1. Ask questions with "Are there any . . .?"
   Answer with 'some' or 'not any'
   a) policemen   b) demonstrators
   c) soldiers   d) tourists
   e) reporters   f) birds
2. Now ask questions with "How many . . . are there?"
   Answer with 'a few' or 'quite a few'

3

This strike began last week and it is still going on. There are some policemen and strikers in front of the factory but only a few. It is Saturday and most of the men are watching a big football match. The strange thing is that there are not any reporters or television cameramen there; perhaps they are at the match too.

1. Ask questions with 'any'
   a) strikers   b) policemen
   c) T.V. cameramen   d) soldiers
2. Are there a few or quite a few people here?
3. Where are all the others?

5

There are quite a few men in this pub. There are also a few women. It is almost closing-time (11 o'clock). The man looking at his wallet is called Fred Collins. He wants some more beer. The trouble is he has not got any money.

1. Ask questions with "Are there any . . . ?"
   or "Is there any . . . ?"
   a) men   b) women
   c) money in Fred's wallet
2. What is Fred doing and why?

2

Susan is going to bake a cake. She has some eggs, butter, sugar and milk. She wants to use only a few eggs and a little butter. She always uses a lot of sugar. She has not got any chocolate. She needs some. It is going to be a chocolate cake.

1. What is Susan going to do?
2. Ask questions with 'any'
   a) eggs   b) butter
   c) sugar   d) milk
3. What does she need? What hasn't she got? Why does she need it?
4. Ask "How much/many . . . is she going to use?"

4

Arthur ordered a steak with some salad and potatoes. The waiter brought him some salad with his steak a few seconds ago but he did not bring him any potatoes. Arthur is telling him to bring him some now. There are only a few people in the restaurant. Perhaps it is not very good.

1. Ask what Arthur ordered and what the waiter brought him!
2. What is Arthur telling him and why?
3. Ask how many people there are!

1 Study this. Notice when we use *is a*, *is some*, and *are some*:

There *is a*	piece of bread packet of butter bottle of milk cigarette detective	over there

There *is some*	bread butter milk tobacco	over there

There *are some*	pieces of bread packets of butter bottles of milk cigarettes detectives	over there

Now use one of these three models for these words

i) oil	v) warm clothes	ix) hot water
ii) tins of oil	vi) warm jacket	x) food
iii) glass of wine	vii) police dog	xi) sandwich
iv) hot coffee	viii) policemen	xii) sandwiches

2 Study the use of *any* in:

a) Negative sentences

There	is not any	food wine money	left
	are not any	sandwiches potatoes cigars	

b) Questions

Is there any	food wine money	left?
Are there any	sandwiches potatoes cigars	

a) Use these tables to make more sentences of your own. b) Make sentences with these words:

i) I didn't use	iii) They didn't want	v) Did she buy
ii) Have you got	iv) Did you get	vi) She didn't buy

3 Study the use of 'a little' and 'a few'

There is We have got	only a little	work time money petrol butter

There are We have got	only a few	cinemas good hotels cheap restaurants here intelligent people big factories

Can you make some sentences of your own, with words like: beef in this beef soup, good book-shops here, parks in Birmingham, wine in the bottle?

THE MAN WHO ESCAPED
Episode 5

SYNOPSIS: *Coke escaped from prison and hid in a field. It was very cold and he knew he had to find warm clothes and food somewhere. He saw a house in the country, isolated and far away from the nearest town. He stood outside the house before going in. He could not understand why there was no noise coming from it, not even the sound of a radio or television.*

1 Coke listened for several seconds but he could not hear anything at all. And yet there was smoke coming from the chimney and there was a light on in the front room! "Why is it so quiet? Is it a trap? Are the police waiting for me in there?" he asked himself. He went to the front door and pushed it. To his surprise it was open! He went in very quietly. 5 In the front room there was a fire burning in the fireplace. The room was clean, small and very warm. There was very little furniture in it– only a couch and a table in front of the fire and two old-fashioned chairs. There were also some photographs on the shelf above the fire. They were yellow and old. One of them was of a young man in a World 10 War I uniform. There were also a few of the same young man and also a woman in old-fashioned wedding-clothes.

2 Suddenly Coke froze. There was someone else in the room. He knew it. He could feel it! He turned around quickly and, at the same time, put his hand in his pocket. There was a small knife there. He saw an 15 old woman. She had a covered dish in her hands and there was a delicious smell of meat and vegetables coming from it. She did not look afraid. She did not even look surprised.
"I'm sorry," she said, and put the dish down on the table.
Coke could hardly believe his ears. Here he was, a stranger in her house 20 and yet she said *she* was sorry!

3 "I'm sorry," she said again. "I didn't hear you. Did you knock? I'm deaf, you see." She pointed to her ear, shook her head and said "deaf" a second time. "People often come to the door and knock, but I don't hear them. I'm glad you came in." 25

Coke stared at her for a second and then finally found his voice. "I . . . I'm sorry. I just stepped in."
He looked down at his clothes. His prison uniform was so dirty that it was impossible to tell what kind of uniform it was. Then he suddenly had an idea. 30

"I'm a mechanic from a garage in town. I came to repair a lorry somewhere out here but the road was icy. I had an accident. I . . . I fell off my motorbike."

He had to say this several times before she finally understood him. When she did, she gave him some hot water and soap and afterwards 35 some food. The only thing he needed now was a change of clothes!

1. Special Transformation Exercise

MODEL: I need some eggs
We haven't got = We haven't got any eggs
cold beer = We haven't got any cold beer

Prompts:

a) sugar   e) I'd like   i) There wasn't
b) There isn't   f) breakfast   j) good films
c) potatoes   g) We didn't have k) I saw
d) coffee   h) rain   l) They went to

2. Conversation

Arthur and his chief engineer, Don Anderson, went to a small town near Manchester last week. They went on business and they had to stay the night in a small hotel. They had to eat in the hotel, too.

DON: Can't we eat somewhere else, Arthur? Very few small hotels like this serve good food.

ARTHUR: I know, but there isn't anywhere else in this town. Besides, the waiter's coming over for our order, now.

WAITER: Good evening. Would you like to order now? I can recommend the roast beef. It's very good.

ARTHUR: No, I'm afraid I don't like roast beef. Let me see . . . what else have you got on your menu. You order first, Don.

DON: All right. Roast beef for me, please. But I don't want any potatoes. I'm trying to lose some weight.

ARTHUR: I think I'd like some fish. Yes, some Scotch salmon, please.

WAITER: Er . . . I'm afraid we haven't got any salmon this evening, sir. The roast beef's really very good indeed, sir.

ARTHUR: No. If I can't have any salmon, I'd like some trout.

WAITER: I'm terribly sorry, sir, but I'm afraid we . . . er . . .

ARTHUR: You mean you haven't got any trout, either!

WAITER: No, sir. I'm afraid not, sir.

ARTHUR: Well . . . hmm . . . I suppose you have some Dover sole, then?

WAITER: Dover sole, sir? Did you say Dover sole, sir?

ARTHUR: Yes, that's right, I'd like some Dover sole with some . . .

WAITER: There's very little good Dover sole on the market at this time of the year, sir. Our roast beef's much better!

ARTHUR: I'm sure it is, but I don't like roast beef. I'd still like . . .

WAITER: Try the roast beef, sir.

ARTHUR: Why? I don't like roast beef! I never eat roast beef! In fact, I hate roast beef!

WAITER: Well . . . I'm afraid we haven't got anything else, sir.

Questions

1. Where does Don want to eat at the beginning and why can't they do this?
2. Ask and answer these questions:
   a) How many small hotels/good food?
   b) Why/Don/potatoes?
3. Ask and answer why Arthur can't get any
   a) salmon   b) trout   c) Dover sole
4. What does the waiter say about the roast beef?
5. Why doesn't Arthur want it?

e Summary

Focal points in this Unit.

1. When we have an idea of the quantity of something but we do not think it is necessary to give the exact amount, we use *some*. We use *some* in positive sentences, with Mass and Unit words:

Examples:

There are some policemen in the park.
There is some chocolate on the table.

2. When we ask questions about something or a number of things, and we have no idea of the quantity, we use *any:*

Examples:

Is there any food left?
Are there any sandwiches for me?

3. We use *any* (instead of *some*) in negative sentences:

Examples:

There isn't any food left.
There aren't any policemen in the park.

4. 'a few' and 'a little':
   a) *a few* means a small number, and we use it with Unit words–a few policemen/ a few people/a few strikers. We sometimes add the word *only* ('only a few') or *quite*. 'Quite a few people' means 'A lot of people'.
   b) *a little* means 'a small quantity', and we use it with Mass words–a little sugar/a little petrol/a little food. We also add the word *only* ('only a little'), but we rarely add the word *quite*.

f Exercises for homework

1. Ask the questions to the situations on page 27, and do the Special Transformation exercise on page 30.

2. Make statements and ask questions about the following things:

Example:

PROMPT: good detective novels in that shop.
RESPONSE: a) There are some good detective novels in that shop.
          b) Are there any good detective novels in that shop?

Prompts:
a) money in his bank account
b) bread in the cupboard
c) tomatoes in that box
d) milk in the fridge
e) chairs in the room
f) Russian students at the University
g) petrol in the tank
h) very good Continental restaurants in London
i) cigarettes left in that packet
j) time left

3. **Guided Composition**

Read situations 1 and 3 on page 27 again carefully, and then write about a demonstration last week. Use the prompts and begin with this sentence:

'There was a small demonstration in Hyde Park last week.'
demonstrators/students/policemen//not any soldiers/but/tourists//reporters/but not many//Saturday/most/football match// also/other young people/Park/not interested /demonstration//

4. **Transfer Exercise**

Write 5 true sentences about yourself using *some* and 5 using *any*. Here are two examples:
'I met some friends in the town yesterday.'
'I didn't have any breakfast this morning.'

Unit 6
a

Past tense with 'Ago' and questions with 'How long ago?'

1

(a) When/open?
(b) What/shoppers?
(c) What/sales people?
(d) Where/detective?
(e) What/wear?
(f) Who/watch?

2

(a) What time?
(b) When/close?
(c) shoppers?
(d) detective?
(e) sales people?
(f) When/last one?

3

(a) When/London express?
(b) What/want to know?
(c) What/answer?

4

(a) Why/a hurry?
(b) When/film?
(c) new film?
(d) When/made?
(e) When/Julia/film before?

5

(a) Where/Fred?
(b) Fred's wife's question?
(c) What time?
(d) When/he/work?
(e) How long ago?

6

(a) What time?
(b) When/lecture?
(c) Why/hesitate?
(d) What/lecture on?

32

1

This is a department store. It is open six days a week, from 9 to 5.30. It is closing now. The shoppers are all leaving and the sales people are counting money. The man in the jacket by the door is a detective. He is watching everybody.

1. What kind of store is this?
2. When is it open?
3. What are the shoppers doing?
4. Ask why!
5. What else is happening?

2

It is 6 o'clock now. The store closed half an hour ago. All the shoppers left the store half an hour ago. The detective watched them. Then the sales people counted their money and went home, too. The last one left fifteen minutes ago. That was at 5.45.

1. What did all the shoppers do half an hour ago and why?
2. What did the detective do?
3. What did the sales people do?
4. When did the last one leave?

3

Arthur thought the London express left at 11.10. In fact it left at 11.05. It left before he got to the station. "How long ago did it leave?" he wants to know. "Five minutes ago, at 11.05" is the answer.

1. What time is it now?
2. What happened before Arthur got to the station?
3. When did he think it left?
4. Ask two questions about the train with
   a) When   b) How long ago

4

Julia and her boyfriend are in a hurry. The film started fifteen minutes ago. They do not want to miss too much of it. It is one of Charles Kay's old horror films. It was made 10 years ago. Julia does not remember but she saw the film on television a few months ago.

1. Ask and answer why Julia and her boyfriend are in a hurry!
2. Ask how long ago the film began!
3. How long ago was it made? What year was that?
4. What is it that Julia does not remember?

5

Fred Collins spends most of his time in pubs. We met him in Unit 5. This is his wife. "I wonder where Fred is?" she is saying. Actually she has a pretty good idea. It is 8 o'clock now and she knows he always leaves work at 5.30. How long ago was that?

1. Is Fred at home?
2. What is his wife saying?
3. Ask these questions about Fred
   a) most of his time   b) When/work
   c) How long ago/work
4. Where do you think Fred is?

6

Tom does not know whether to go to the lecture or not. It is already 3.15 and it started at 3. How long ago was that? Tom is hesitating because he does not want to disturb anyone in the hall. The lecture is on language-teaching.

1. Ask two questions about the lecture:
   a) When   b) How long ago
2. Ask what Tom is doing and why!
3. What is the lecture on?
4. Make a sentence of your own with 'didn't know whether to . . . or not'.

FORMATION AND MANIPULATION

---

1 Notice that the word *ago* comes after phrases like 'fifteen minutes', 'half an hour', '10 years'.

A	B	C	D
They	left	the cinema	half an hour	ago

  i) How many words can you think of to replace 'They' in box A? (for example: 'he').
 ii) Now think of words to replace 'the cinema' in box B.
iii) Now look at the situations on page 33 and find other time phrases to replace 'half an hour'.
 iv) Make as many sentences as you can using the words you have for exercises i), ii) and iii).

---

2 Notice the question form with *How long ago*.

A	B	C
How long ago did	the film	start?

  i) Find as many words as you can to replace 'the film' in box B and 'start' in box C.
 ii) Now ask questions with the words you have from exercise i, and with the words you have from exercise **1** iii, answer them like this:

> *Question:* How long ago did they go home?
> *Answer:* Ten minutes ago.

---

3 Verbs like *start, arrive* and *wash* are regular verbs. They end in *-ed* in the past: *started, arrived* and *washed*.
Verbs like *leave, see* and *read* are irregular and have different types of past forms: *left, saw* and *read*.

---

4 **You must learn the past forms of regular and irregular verbs by heart. There is a list of verbs at the back of this book. Learn five verbs each day. Start today and learn these verb-forms**

do – did	get – got	find – found
start – started	look – looked	

THE MAN WHO ESCAPED
Episode 6

SYNOPSIS: *After Coke escaped, he hid in a field all day. Then, when it got dark, he went into a small house in the country. There was an old deaf lady in the house. She gave him food. The young detective who arrested Coke four years ago, Baxter, left London by train. Scotland Yard's orders were "Find Coke immediately!"*

1   It was a cold and miserable night. Only a few miles away from the house Coke was in, two policemen in a small village police station could hear the wind outside. One of them was a sergeant. The other was much younger.
"I wonder how Mrs Bentley is?" the sergeant asked.   5
"Mrs Bentley? Oh, you mean that old lady whose husband died a few years ago?"
"That's right. She's deaf, you know, so she never listens to the radio or watches television. In fact, she doesn't even read the papers."
"Oh?" the young policeman said. He wondered why the sergeant   10
wanted to tell him all this. Then he found out.
"Why don't you go out to her place and see if she's all right?"
"Who? Me? On a night like this?"
"It's not far. Besides, you've got your bike, haven't you?"

2   Baxter got off the train at a small station. There was a detective waiting   15
for him on the platform. He shook Baxter's hand.
"My name's Halls, Tom Halls. Scotland Yard phoned us and told us to meet you here. There's a car waiting."
Baxter wasted very little time on social formalities.
"Coke escaped more than 24 hours ago. I want to catch him before   20
another 24 hours are up."
Halls looked at Baxter for a few seconds before he answered.
"A lot of us wonder why Scotland Yard is so interested in this fellow Coke. He isn't the first one to escape. Another man did only about six months ago, but Scotland Yard didn't send anyone to help us then."   25
Baxter was already half-way to the car before he said anything.
"Coke isn't just an ordinary prisoner. He's very special. Let's get going!"

3   The young policeman was angry. He was on the road now. The wind was cold and blew snow into his face. "That stupid sergeant!" he   30
thought. "We must be one of the last stations in England that still uses bikes, and he sends me out on one on a night like this!"
He had to get off the bike and push it up a hill. It was the last hill between the station and the old lady's house. When he got to the top of it he could see the house down below, at the bottom of the hill. Just   35
as he looked down at it, he saw a light go on in one of the rooms up-stairs. "Stupid! That's what it is, sending me out on a night like this!" the policeman said again. Then he got on his bike and began to go down the hill very fast, towards the house.

Unit 6
d

1. Invention Exercise

This exercise practises the Past tense with *ago*, but we have also added the words *first* and *last*. Notice where we put these words in the Model. *First* here means 'the first time', *last* means 'the last time'.

Make sentences using the prompts:

Example:

MODEL: I $\begin{Bmatrix}\text{first}\\\text{last}\end{Bmatrix}$ went to London 10 years ago.

PROMPT: She first/Buckingham Palace/3 years

RESPONSE: She first saw Buckingham Palace 3 years ago.

or: She first visited Buckingham Palace 3 years ago.

Prompts:

a) She last/London/3 weeks
b) They first/the cinema/25 years
c) I last/him/five minutes
d) We last/champagne/at a party/a fortnight
e) Tom and Susan last/a wine and cheese party/about 6 weeks
f) He first/a pipe/10 years
g) I first/a novel by Nevil Shute/6 years
h) She first/a television programme/3 years
i) Arthur last/a new car/2 months
j) That man first/to prison/25 years

2. Conversation

Arthur Tigers went out to lunch at 12 o'clock. It's now 2.30 and he's just walking into his office. His secretary is typing. Before Arthur went to lunch, he told his secretary, Miss Bradley, to ring him at the restaurant if a man called Mr Powell came to see him. Arthur came back from lunch only a second ago.

MISS BRADLEY: (nervously) Good afternoon, Mr Tigers. Did you have a good lunch?

ARTHUR: Yes, thank you, Miss Bradley. It was very good. Did anyone phone while I was out?

MISS BRADLEY: No. Nobody phoned, but . . . er . . . Mr Powell came.

ARTHUR: What? But he's the man I told you about!

MISS BRADLEY: Yes, I know, but . . .

ARTHUR: Well, if you knew, why didn't you phone me? Mr Powell has some very important information. I wanted to talk to him as soon as possible. I told you all that before I left. Didn't you understand me?

MISS BRADLEY: Yes, of course, I understood you, Mr Tigers, but . . .

ARTHUR: I even gave you a card with the name and phone number of the restaurant! I put it on your desk.

MISS BRADLEY: But that's just it! You didn't give me the card. You didn't put it on my desk!

ARTHUR: What do you mean? Of course I did. I took the card out of my wallet just before I went to lunch! Look! It isn't in my wallet now! (suddenly) Oh!

MISS BRADLEY: Mr Tigers, what's that card on the floor? It fell out of your wallet a second ago.

ARTHUR: That card? It's . . . er . . . it's the card I thought I gave you.

MISS BRADLEY: You see! You forgot! That's why I didn't phone. I didn't know where you were.

ARTHUR: No. I'm very sorry, Miss Bradley. It wasn't your fault. I apologise.

MISS BRADLEY: That's all right. Please forget it.

Questions

1. Ask (and answer) when Mr Powell came!
2. Why is Arthur so angry when Miss Bradley tells him this?
3. What does Arthur think he did before he left? Ask and answer if he did! (her the card. on her desk)
4. Why didn't Miss Bradley phone Arthur?
5. What are Arthur's exact words when he apologises?
6. What is one thing we can say in English when someone apologises to us?

Practice

Which form of these words do we use in questions in the past? Which form do we use in statements about the past? Make sentences with each!

a) have/had
b) tell/told
c) phone/phoned
d) understand/understood
e) give/gave
f) know/knew
g) forget/forgot
h) go/went
i) come/came
j) fall/fell

e   Summary

Focal points in this Unit.

1. The word *ago* goes after phrases like 'two minutes', 'three years', 'a long time', 'half an hour', and means a certain time ('two minutes', 'three years' etc) *back from now*. Remember and look at the examples you have learned in this Unit:

    'It is 6 o'clock now. The store closed at 5.30. That was *half an hour ago*.'

2. Use the Simple Past tense with the word *ago*:

    'It *left* 5 minutes *ago*'/'The film *was made* 10 years *ago*.'/'Arthur *came* back from lunch only a second *ago*.'

3. To ask a question with *ago*, we often use 'How long ago . . .?':

    '*How long ago* did it leave?'/'*How long ago* was that?'

4. Remember how we use the two words *first* and *last* with the Simple Past and *ago*. Look at the Invention Exercise on page 36 again. Here is one example to remind you:

    'I *last* saw him 5 minutes ago.'

f   Exercises for homework

1. Do all the exercises and questions on pages 33 and 34.

2. Ask and answer questions using *ago*.

    Example:

    It is 8 o'clock and I am watching television. I turned it on at 7.

    You write:

    Q: How long ago did you turn the television on?
    A: I turned it on an hour ago.

    a) It's March now, and Mary is living in France. She went to France in January.

    b) It's 4.30 now, and Arthur is sitting in his office. He came back from lunch at 2.30.

    c) Tony is standing outside a shop (It's 6.30). But the shop closed at 5.30.

    d) It's 3 o'clock, and Deborah is sitting in the airport lounge looking sad. Her plane left for Paris at 1 o'clock.

    e) Tony is staying at the Hilton Hotel. (It's January, 1970) He last stayed there in July, 1969.

3. **Guided Composition**

    Read the conversation again on page 36. Mr Powell came while Arthur was at lunch. Write the short conversation between Mr Powell and Arthur's secretary, using the following prompts:

    MR POWELL: afternoon//Mr Tigers?//
    MISS BRADLEY: afternoon//No/lunch/half an hour//
    MR POWELL: Where?//important information //must/soon as possible//
    MISS BRADLEY: don't know where//told me/no address or phone number//Mr Tigers/not/ card//sorry//
    MR POWELL: all right//not/fault//tell/ring later//Good bye.
    MISS BRADLEY: really/sorry//tell Mr Tigers// Good bye.

4. **Transfer Exercise**

    Write 5 or more true sentences about yourself, friends or relations, using the word *ago*.

    Example:

    I left school 5 years ago.
    My parents and I spent 2 months in Italy 3 years ago.

Unit 7

a   Adjectives and adverbs

1

(a) How/tall player?
(b) How/short player?
(c) What/ yesterday?
(d) won?
(e) lost?

2

(a) Where/ yesterday?
(b) beginning?
(c) end of the film?
(d) Why/in the middle?
(e) Where/Arthur and Deborah?
(f) Why/walk out?

3

'Parlez Vous Français?'

MISS EUROPE

"Sprechen Sie Deutsch"

(a) How/piano?
(b) How/tennis?
(c) good cook?
(d) How/French and German?

4

POLICE

(a) Fred/bus-driver?
(b) Why/3 accidents?
(c) worst accident?
(d) What/after that?

5

about 45 hours a week

60 hours a week

COMPANY DIRECTOR

(a) How/Arthur/ when/younger?
(b) How many hours?
(c) How/now?
(d) How many hours/now?

6

R. CARTER BUILDER

J. FLASH
HOUSES FOR YOU

(a) What/Carter and Flash do?
(b) How/houses?
(c) Why/man/ shout?

> She's a GOOD singer. She sings WELL.
> He works AS HARD AS his father did.
> He drove SO DANGEROUSLY THAT he lost his job.

1

These two often play tennis. The tall player is good. He is playing well. The short one is bad. He is playing badly. One always wins and the other always loses. They also played yesterday. Who do you think won? Who lost?

1. What do these two often do?
2. Ask a question about 'now'!
3. What kind of a player is the tall one?
4. How is he playing?
5. Ask the same questions about the other!
6. What happened yesterday?

2

Julia and her boyfriend went to a film yesterday. They missed the beginning and they did not see the end. It was so bad that they walked out in the middle.

Deborah and Arthur went to the opera. The singers sang so badly that they walked out too.

1. Ask these questions about Julia and her boyfriend:
   a) What/yesterday   b) the beginning
   c) the end   d) Why/in the middle
2. Ask what Deborah and Arthur did!
3. How did the singers sing?

3

Carol Stuart plays the piano and tennis very well. She is a very good cook and swimmer. She speaks French and German perfectly. She is beautiful, too. That is why she was Miss Europe last year.

1. Ask how well she does these things:
   a) tennis   b) the piano
   c) French   d) German
2. Make sentences with 'good' or 'well' about her with these words:
   a) swimmer   b) swims
   c) cooks   d) a cook

4

Fred Collins used to be a bus driver but he is not any more. He drove so badly and dangerously that he had three accidents in one month. The worst was when he ran into a police car. He lost his job after that.

1. Is Fred still a bus driver?
2. What can you say about Fred
   a) as a driver   b) the way he drove?
3. Ask how many accidents he had! (answer)
4. What was the worst and what happened after that?

5

When Sir Arthur was younger he worked very hard. He worked at least 60 hours a week and always did a lot of work. He still works hard but not quite as hard as he used to. He works about 45 hours a week now.

Ask these questions and answer them:
   a) How many hours/ b) How many now?
      younger?
   c) hard then? hard   d) hard as he used to?
      now?

6

R. Carter and J. Flash both build houses but Carter builds them much better. He is a much better builder. Flash builds houses quickly but badly. Once he built a house in a week. It fell down a week later. The man shouting at Flash is the man who bought the house.

1. What can you say about Carter's houses and also the way he builds them?
2. How does Flash build his houses?
3. What happened once?
4. Who is the other man in the picture shouting at Flash?

1 Study this. Notice how we use the words *good* and *bad*, and *well* and *badly*. Notice too their position in the sentence

He			tennis player
	is a	good	teacher
		bad	swimmer
She			driver

He		plays tennis	
	teaches	well
	swims	badly
She	drives	

i) Make pairs of sentences from the tables above.
   Example: 'She's a bad driver. She drives badly.'
ii) Make pairs of sentences in the same way with these prompts:
   Example: French speaker = 'He's a good French speaker. He speaks French well.'
   piano-player: builder: singer: cook: typist.

2 Notice how we form adverbs from adjectives. There are three main types:
   i) Adverbs made from an adjective + *ly* or *ily:*
   quick – quickly   angry – angrily
   careful – carefully   noisy – noisily
   dangerous – dangerously   easy – easily
   ii) Adverbs which have the same form as the adjective:
   hard – hard   fast – fast
   iii) Adverbs which are completely different from the adjective:
                            good – well
   Ask another student about himself, his (or her) friends or relatives using some of the adverbs
   above.
   Example: Does your father work very hard?
            Do you drive very carefully?

3

	A	B	C	D
	He	drove so dangerously	that	he lost his job

i) Think of words to replace 'drove' and 'dangerously' in box B.
ii) Now, with another student, ask and answer questions like this:
   Question: How dangerously did he drive?
   Answer: So dangerously that he lost his job.

4

	A	B	C
	He doesn't work	as hard as	he used to

i) Think of words to replace 'hard' in box B.
ii) Now write four sentences using this structure.

THE MAN WHO ESCAPED
Episode 7

SYNOPSIS: *Coke found food in a small house in the country. Baxter arrived at a small station. Another detective met him there and asked Baxter why Scotland Yard was so interested in Coke. A sergeant in a police station not far from the house Coke was in sent a young policeman to the house to tell the old lady in it about Coke.*

1 "You know, your clothes are in a terrible state," the old lady said after the meal. "You ruined them when you had the accident!"
"That's all right. They're just my work-clothes," Coke answered.
"My husband was just about your size. A little heavier perhaps. All his clothes are upstairs. They're no good to him. He died two years 5 ago." She pointed up to the room above them.
"Why don't you see if any of his clothes fit you. You can bring them back tomorrow."
"Nobody can be this lucky!" Coke thought to himself. He went upstairs and turned the light on. It was clear that the old lady was almost 10 in another world. She trusted everybody. He found a heavy jacket, a woollen shirt and some trousers hanging in the room.

2 "What do you know about Coke?" Baxter asked Halls. They were in the car now. "Very little, I'm afraid. In fact, I don't think I know anything about him at all. Wasn't he the fellow who was in that spy case about 15 four years ago?"
"Yes, that's right. Coke always said it wasn't him . . . that it was someone else."
"That's what they all say. But what's so special about him?"
"Coke was in Army Intelligence. He knew important secrets. We 20 could never understand why he sold them. There wasn't a real motive. Some said he did it for money. We couldn't prove it, but if he was a spy, he still knows too much. We could never find out who he sold the secrets to. That's why we have to catch him before he makes contact with any of his old friends!" 25

3 Coke put the clothes on as quickly as he could. They were old and shabby, but at least they were warm. When he came downstairs, the old lady was still in front of the fire. She smiled when she looked at him.
"You know, you look just like my husband in those clothes . . . when he was much younger, of course." 30
Coke tried to be polite. He wanted to leave quickly.
"I can't thank you enough. It's very kind of you to do all this for me."
The old lady did not seem to hear him.
"Just like my husband," she said again. Just then, there was a knock on the door. 35

1. Invention Exercise

1) Make your own sentences with the pattern:
So good/bad, etc. that
MODEL: The film was so bad that they
walked out in the middle.

Example:

PROMPT: film/interesting/twice
RESPONSE: The film was so interesting that I
saw it twice.

Prompts:

a) weather/cold/two sweaters
b) football match/bad/in the middle
c) music/loud/a headache
d) service in the restaurant/slow/out
e) lecture/uninteresting/out
f) book/good/3 times

2) Now make sentences with the pattern: So
well/badly, etc. that
MODEL: The short man played so badly
that he lost the match.

Example:

PROMPT: Fred/dangerously/his job
RESPONSE: Fred drove so dangerously that he
lost his job.

Prompts:

a) orchestra/badly/out
b) she/piano/well/a prize
c) man/carelessly/3 accidents in a week
d) athlete/slowly/the race
e) Flash/house/badly/down
f) boss/hard/ill

2. Conversation

Susan used the car today. She drove Tom to
college this morning and then went to her
mother's house. She is driving Tom back from
the college now.

TOM: Why are you driving so slowly?
SUSAN: I'm going as fast as the speed-limit.
TOM: You can forget the speed-limit. Nobody
drives that slowly!

SUSAN: Well, I want to drive carefully. The
roads are crowded.
TOM: But they were just as crowded this
morning. You drove a lot faster then!
SUSAN: That's just it. I drove too fast.
TOM: What? You mean something happened
after you left me?
SUSAN: (nervously) It was in the centre of
town. I was in a hurry, and . . .
TOM: Yes? Go on! What happened?
SUSAN: A child ran out in front of me.
TOM: You mean . . . you mean . . .
SUSAN: Wait! Listen! The girl was a good
distance away so I didn't slow down.
TOM: (relieved) Well, what's so terrible about
that?
SUSAN: Just a second. There's more. The child
fell down.
TOM: Fell down? You mean you hit her?
SUSAN: No, but I almost did. I braked as hard
as I could. I stopped, but only just in time.
TOM: Well, at least you didn't have an
accident!
SUSAN: No, but that isn't the only reason I'm
driving so carefully.
TOM: Oh, no! Did something else happen?
SUSAN: No, but there's a police car behind us.
It's following us, so we can't forget the
speed-limit, can we?

Correct the statements

'The roads were not as crowded this morning.'
'No, the roads were just as crowded this
morning.'
1) Susan is driving very fast now.
2) She drove very slowly this morning.
3) A dog ran out in front of Susan.
4) The child was not very far away.
5) Nothing happened when the child ran
across the road.
6) When the child fell, Susan did not do
anything.
7) Susan is driving slowly and carefully only
because she wants to.

e   Summary

Focal points in this Unit.

1. Adjectives (*good, bad, careful, noisy*) are used with nouns and come before the noun: 'He's *a good worker*'/'She's *a careful driver*'. Adverbs (*well, badly, carefully, noisily*) are used after the verb and answer the question '*How* does he work?': 'He *works carefully*'.

2. Most adverbs are formed by adding *-ly* to the adjective. Notice how certain things change in the spelling:

   a) quick–quickly   (adjective–*ly*)
   b) careful–carefully ('l'–*lly*)
   c) terrible–terribly   ('ble'–*bly*)
   d) angry–angrily   ('y'–*ily*)

3. Some adverbs have exactly the same form as the adjective:

   hard; fast; early; late.

4. Remember particularly the irregular *good–well*.

5. Use the pattern 'He . . . *so (badly/carelessly etc.)* that he . . .' when you want to show the result of an action:

   'He drove carelessly. + He lost his job.'
   ='He drove *so carelessly that* he lost his job.'

6. Use the pattern *as . . . as* to compare how two people do (or did) the same thing:

   'He doesn't work quite *as hard as* his father did.'

f   Exercises for homework

1. Do all the exercises and questions on pages 39 and 40.

2. **Transformation Exercise**

   Example:

   He works hard. His father worked hard, too.
   You write:
   He works as hard as his father did.

   a) The new girl types well. The old secretary typed well, too.
   b) You speak French fluently. Your teacher spoke fluently, too.
   c) He works fast. His father worked fast, too.
   d) That boy writes carefully. His brother wrote carefully, too.
   e) He talks loudly. The other teacher talked loudly, too.

3. **Guided Composition**

   Read situation 4 on page 39 again carefully, and then write about this person:

   Mary/shorthand-typist/American firm/any more//badly/carelessly/at least 10 mistakes/ every letter//worst/30 mistakes/letter for the boss//lost/job//

4. **Transfer Exercise**

   Write 5 true sentences about yourself, relatives or friends using the patterns '*so . . . that*' and '*as . . . as*':

   Example:

   My father speaks French so well that people sometimes think he is French.
   My friend works as quickly as I do.

1

(a) Which man/ harder?

(b) man with shovel/more money/ tractor driver?

2

(a) How/both drivers?

(b) How/driver number 3/ drive?

(c) Who/win?

3

(a) Who/best job?

(b) Who/hardest?

(c) Who/most money?

4

(a) How/ski?

(b) Who/worse?

(c) What/the man?

(d) both beginners?

5

(a) What/both men?

(b) evening?

(c) Why/more clearly?

6

(a) How/when younger?

(b) What/one day?

(c) What/old lady?

(d) How/Tom/ now?

1

One of these men is a tractor driver. The man with the shovel is an ordinary worker. They both have to work hard, but one of them has to work a bit harder than the other. Which of them do you think it is? The man with the shovel, by the way, earns less money than the tractor driver.

1. Correct the statements!
   a) Only one of the men has to work hard.
   b) The tractor driver earns less than the other man does.
2. Ask and answer the questions!
   a) tractor driver/hard?
   b) as hard as the other man?

2

Both these drivers are good. Both have fast cars but one of them is driving a bit better and faster than the other is. We cannot be sure which of them is going to win the race, but it looks as if number three is going to.

1. Ask and answer the questions!
   a) both/good   b) both/well
2. What can you say about one of them?
3. Correct the statements!
   a) The driver of three is not driving as well or as fast as seven is.
   b) We can be sure that three is going to win the race.

3

The man with the watch never has to work as hard as the other two do. He has the best job of the three. He earns the most money and does the least work. The man with the shovel has the worst job. He works the hardest but earns the least.

1. Correct the statements!
   a) The man with the watch has to work harder than the other two do.
   b) He earns the least money and does the most work.
2. Who do you think has the worst job? Why?

4

Neither Tom nor Susan can ski very well. They are both ski-ing very badly at the moment, but she is ski-ing even worse than he is. At least he is managing to keep his balance. It is hard for both of them. They are both beginners.

1. Correct the statements!
   a) Both Tom and Susan can ski well.
   b) She is ski-ing a bit better than he is.
2. Why can we say Tom is ski-ing better?
3. Why is it hard for both of them?

5

Both of these men are looking at the moon but neither of them can see it very clearly. It is a rather cloudy evening. One of the men can see the moon just a bit more clearly than the other can because he has a much bigger telescope.

1. Ask and answer!
   a) What/looking at?   b) clear evening?
   c) very clearly?   d) Which man/more clearly?
2. Ask why one can see it more clearly than the other! (and answer)

6

Tom drives a lot more carefully than he did when he was younger. He almost ran over an old lady one day. He just missed her. She managed to get out of the way just in time. He drives much more carefully now than he used to.

1. Correct the statements!
   a) Tom ran over an old lady one day.
   b) She did not get out of the way.
   c) Tom still drives very dangerously.

Unit 8

b

FORMATION AND MANIPULATION

FORMATION AND MANIPULATION

1 Pronunciation

REMEMBER: *than* is pronounced [ðən]

Example: Planes now fly faster [ðən] they used to

2 He drives dangerously, but . . .

A	B	C	D	E
she drives	more	dangerously	than	he does

i) Put the words 'careful', 'quick', 'slow' in their correct forms into box C.

ii) Make sentences beginning 'He drives dangerously, but . . .' (Remember you can also put other words into box E in place of *he*)

3 He works well/fast/hard/badly, but . . .
(Make sentences)

she works you work they work	better faster harder worse	*than* [ðən]	he does

4

That man has	the best the worst	job
He does	the least the most	work

Make sentences with: job, house, car, *and* money, time, fun

5 These words are like dangerously, carefully, etc. (See **2** above)–clearly, loudly, weakly, heavily.

46

THE MAN WHO ESCAPED
Episode 8

SYNOPSIS: *After Coke escaped from prison, he found a small house several miles away from the nearest village. The old lady in the house gave him food and clothes. She was deaf. A policeman came out to her house to tell her to look out for Coke.*

1   The deaf old lady did not hear the knock, but Coke did. His heart began to pound wildly. Whoever it was obviously knew there was someone inside because there was a light on and smoke coming from the chimney. He had to decide what to do, and quickly.
"There's someone at the door", he said loudly, but the old lady did   5
not understand.
"There's someone at the door", he said again, this time even more loudly than before. She went out of the room and Coke quickly stepped back into the shadows of the front room.

2   The old lady opened the front door. Coke could see her quite clearly,   10
but nothing else. He listened carefully.
"Hello, Mrs Bentley. I'm from the village police station. The sergeant sent me. I've got something to tell you."
Then Coke saw the policeman very clearly. Coke looked around quickly. There was a poker lying in the fireplace. He almost went to get it and   15
then stopped.
"No!" he thought "That's too dangerous. They already think I'm a spy. Whatever I have to do I can do just as well with my fists." He stepped back and waited. The old lady and the policeman came through the door into the sitting-room. Coke was still behind the door, so the   20
policeman could not see him.
"Good evening officer. Can I help you?" Coke said very loudly and clearly. The policeman turned around and looked at Coke. He was very surprised. Then Coke hit him as hard as he could in the stomach and he fell to the floor heavily. The old lady screamed. The policeman   25
tried to get up, but fell back weakly. Coke ran out of the room.

3   The phone rang about five minutes later at the local police headquarters. Halls answered it.
"What? Coke? Where? When?"
Baxter stood up as soon as he heard Coke's name. He quickly put his   30
hat and coat on. Halls listened carefully to the voice on the other end and quickly made a few notes. Then he put the phone down and turned to Baxter.
"Well, we know where Coke is now. A policeman almost caught him only five minutes ago."   35
"What do you mean, 'he almost caught him'? Did he catch him or didn't he?"
"No, he got away. He stole the policeman's bike."

47

Unit 8
d

FURTHER PRACTICE

1. For Comprehension

Read this short report, and then answer the questions.

A British university is now doing research into the difference between men and women drivers. It seems that women often drive more carefully than men. The research suggests that men drive faster and more recklessly, but that they also react a bit faster in emergencies. This is perhaps because it seems they concentrate more when they are driving.

Correct these statements (Notice the use of *less* here!):

a) It seems that men drive more slowly than women do.
b) Men drive less recklessly than women do.
c) Men react more slowly than women do in emergencies.
d) Men concentrate less when driving than women do.

Now give full answers to these questions:

e) What is the university mentioned doing research into?
f) What does the research suggest is the difference in the way men and women drive?
g) What does it suggest is the difference in emergencies?
h) Why is this?

2. Conversation

Tom and Susan spent a few days in London last month. They left their car at home and stayed in a good hotel in the centre of town. They spent a lot of money. This is what happened the day they went home.

SUSAN: Why do we have to walk to the station? And where is it?
TOM: It's just down that road . . . I think.
SUSAN: Look! There's a policeman! Ask him the way.
TOM: All right. Excuse me. Can you tell me the way to Waterloo Station?
POLICEMAN: Yes. Walk down this road, take the first turning on the left. Then walk until you come to the river and . . .
TOM: The river?
POLICEMAN: Yes. You can't see it very clearly from here. When you come to it, there's a bridge. Just walk across it. Follow the signs

that say 'To Waterloo Station'. You can't miss it.
TOM: And is it very far? I mean, how long does it take to walk there?
POLICEMAN: About fifteen minutes, if you walk quickly.
TOM: I see. Thank you very much.
POLICEMAN: Not at all.
SUSAN: Fifteen minutes! And with these heavy suitcases, too! I think we ought to take a taxi.
TOM: Not at this hour. Look at the traffic. It's moving very slowly. We can get there just as quickly on foot.
SUSAN: Well, I can't possibly carry this case any farther.
TOM: All right. Let me take it, then.
SUSAN: Don't be silly. You can't carry your case and mine as well!
TOM: Yes, I can. The cases aren't that heavy . . . hmm!
SUSAN: You see! They're heavier than you thought!
TOM: Perhaps it's not such a bad idea after all.
SUSAN: What isn't such a bad idea? What do you mean?
TOM: Taxi! Taxi!

Questions

1. What is the first thing Tom asks the policeman?
2. What exactly are the policeman's instructions?
3. How long does he say it takes?
4. What does Susan think they ought to do and why?
5. Why doesn't Tom want to do this?
6. What does Tom find out when he lifts the case?
7. What does he say then and what does he do?

Practice

Practise the pattern CAN YOU TELL ME THE WAY TO . . .? with someone else. Think of places you both know. Ask the other person questions with the pattern. Then the other person must tell you how to get there, using such phrases as 'Walk down/up . . .', 'Walk until you come to a . . .' and 'Take the first/the second/the third turning on the . . .' (Notice that you say *Drive* if you are talking to someone in a car)

e   Summary

Focal points in this Unit.

1. Remember that *than* is pronounced [ðen].

2. Remember the way we form and use adverbs when comparing things:

   a) 'He drives *more carefully than* you do.'
   b) 'She works *faster than* he does.'
   c) 'He plays tennis *worse/better than* I do.'

3. Remember the Superlative forms we have used in this Unit:

   a) 'He gets *the most* money and works *the least*.'
   b) 'He has *the best/the worst* house.'

4. We can add the words *a bit, much, rather* or *far* to a Comparative:

   a) 'They react *a bit faster* in emergencies.'
   b) 'He drives *much more carefully* now than he used to.'

f Exercises for homework

1. Do all the exercises on pages 45 and 48.

2. Fill in the correct form of the word in brackets in these sentences:

   Example:

   Maria sings . . . than Julia does. (good)
   You write: *better*, because this is the form of the word needed here.

   a) He plays the violin much . . . than John does. (good)
   b) Margaret types . . . than Mary does. (fast)
   c) He's a . . . driver. He had another accident last week. (careless)
   d) This case is . . . than I thought. (heavy)
   e) This new chair is extremely . . . (comfortable)
   f) Haven't you got a . . . book than that. (interesting)
   g) I can't see it very . . . . (clear)

h) You're walking very . . . today! (slow)
i) They say that men drive . . . and . . . than women do. (fast) (reckless)

3. Use the model and write more sentences of your own using the prompts:

   MODEL: He drives *much more carefully* now than he used to.
   PROMPTS: sing/good
   You write: *She sings much better now than she used to.*

   Prompts:
   a) play/good   f) work/hard
   b) eat/slow   g) drive/careless
   c) speak English/fluent h) dance/bad
   d) work/careful   i) go to bed/late
   e) speak/clear

4. **Guided Composition**

   Read the conversation between Tom and Susan again (page 48), and then write a conversation between a man who is lost and a policeman, using the prompts:

   MAN: Excuse//way/the Central Hotel?//
   POLICEMAN: Pardon?
   MAN: way/Central Hotel?//stranger here//
   POLICEMAN: Yes.//that road/second turning/right//Then until/traffic lights . . .
   MAN: Traffic lights?
   POLICEMAN: Yes.//not very clearly//When/first turning/right//not miss//
   MAN: very far?//how long/walk there?//
   POLICEMAN: 10 minutes/quickly//
   MAN: see//Thank you//

5. **Transfer Exercise**

   Now write some true sentences about yourself or your relations or friends.
   Use this model:

   I . . . much more . . . ly than I used to.
   He . . . far . . . er than he used to.

   Examples:

   My brother writes much better than he used to.
   I drive far more carefully than I used to.
   My sister types much faster than she used to.

1

(a) When/land/ on the moon?

(b) stay/long?

(c) When/take off?

(d) astronauts/ inside?

(e) walk on the moon

2

(a) What/Fred/a few seconds?

(b) When/wife?

(c) Where/wife/ now?

(d) Fred's wife/ do

3

(a) What/Julia and boyfriend?

(b) What/fastest way?

(c) When/train?

(d) What/Julia/ think?

4

(a) What/Tom and Susan?

(b) When/start?

(c) When/guests?

(d) What/Tom want to know?

5

(a) Where/Arthur and Deborah?

(b) When/curtain?

(c) What/ Deborah/say?

6

(a) Why/Julia/ get wet?

(b) What/driver?

1

The spacecraft is going to land on the moon in a few seconds. It is not going to stay there very long. It is going to take off again in 24 hours. Are the astronauts going to stay inside the spacecraft? Or are they going to walk on the moon?

1. Give short answers with 'is/isn't' or 'are/ aren't'.
   a) Is the spacecraft going to take off now?
   b) Is it going to land soon?
   c) Is it going to stay there very long?
2. Ask questions about the astronauts
   a) inside   b) on the moon

2

Fred Collins is going to get a very nasty shock in a few seconds. He does not know that his wife came in only a few seconds ago and is standing behind him. What is she going to do? What do you think the girl with Fred is going to do?

1. What kind of shock is Fred going to get?
2. Ask why (and answer)!
3. Ask a question about Fred's wife with 'When'!
4. Ask and answer a question with 'going to' about the girl!

3

Julia and her boyfriend saw a film in the centre of London this evening. The fastest way home is the train but they are obviously going to miss it. It is going to leave any second. "I'm going to find a boyfriend with a car!" Julia is thinking to herself.

Ask and answer the questions!
1. What/this evening
2. What/fastest way home
3. catch or miss
4. When/leave

4

Tom and Susan are going to give a party this evening. A lot of people are going to come. The party is going to start at 8.30 so the first guests are going to come any minute. "When are you going to take off that apron?" Tom wants to know. "In a minute," is Susan's answer.

1. Ask and answer the questions!
   a) When/a party
   b) start
   c) the guests
2. What is Susan doing and what is she going to do?

5

Arthur and Deborah are at the opera again. The curtain is going to rise and the opera is going to begin in a few seconds. "I hope that woman is going to take off her hat!" Deborah is saying loudly. "We aren't going to see very much if she keeps it on!"

1. Ask and answer the questions!
   a) When/the curtain
   b) the opera/soon
2. What does Deborah hope the woman in front is going to do and why?

6

It is going to rain and Julia hasn't got an umbrella. "I'm going to get very wet if that bus doesn't come soon!" she is saying to herself. She does not know it but the driver of that car is going to stop and he is going to offer her a lift.

1. Ask and answer the questions!
   a) raining now   b) soon
2. What is going to happen if the bus doesn't come soon?
3. What is it that Julia doesn't know?

1 Pronunciation

REMEMBER: the word *to* is often pronounced [tə].

For example: The rocket is going [tə] land on the moon. (Page 51 situation 1)

2

A	B	C	D
He's	going to	come in	soon

i) Think of words to replace 'He's' in box A.

ii) Think of words to replace 'come in' in box C.

iii) Now write five sentences using the words you have for boxes A and C.

3 Very often when we use 'going to' we also say the time. Look at the situations on page 51 and find other time expressions to replace those in **2** box D.

4 Now look at this sentence:

A	B	C	D	E
I'm	not going to	see	him	today

Here are some more time expressions that we use with 'going to':

NOW   TOMORROW   NEXT WEEK   NEXT MONTH

i) Think of words to replace those in boxes A, C, D and E.

ii) Say and write as many sentences as you can using all the words you have for exercise i and Part **3**.

5 Now, make questions (and answer them) using the correct parts of the table above and question words like Where . . .? When . . .? Why . . .? and How . . .?

Example: 'When are you going to meet him?' 'As soon as possible.'

6 *It's going to* (page 51 situation 6)

We talk about what the weather (and other things) are going to do like this:

(Make sentences)

It's going to	rain snow stop thunder	soon in a minute in a little while tomorrow

7 Notice this structure from page 51 situation 6–

(Make sentences)

I'm He's She's	going to	get wet be tired be late	if	the bus the train	doesn't	arrive come soon get here

THE MAN WHO ESCAPED

Episode 9

SYNOPSIS: *Coke found food and clothes in a cottage several miles away from the nearest village. However, a policeman came to tell the old lady in the cottage to watch out for Coke. Coke knocked the policeman down and stole his bike.*

1 Baxter got into the car first. Halls was right behind him. "You drive. You know the area better than I do," Baxter said. They raced out of the town and into the dark countryside.
   "It's ridiculous," Halls said. "Does he really think he's going to get away from us on a bike?"   5
   "Coke isn't a fool," Baxter answered. "He probably doesn't realise we already know what happened in the old lady's house."
   "You mean he doesn't know that even village policemen have small two-way radios these days?"
   "That's right. He probably thinks it's going to take that policeman at   10
least half an hour to get to the nearest phone. He thinks he can get pretty far in that time."

2 Ten minutes later, about three miles from the old lady's house, Baxter suddenly saw someone on the dark road ahead.
   "Look! There!" he shouted. "There's someone on a bike! And look!   15
He's going to get off!"
   Halls saw the man quite clearly, but only for a second. As soon as the man saw they were in a police car, he dropped his bike and ran into the trees at the side of the road.
   "That's Coke!" Baxter shouted. "He isn't going to get away this time!"   20
Baxter jumped out of the car even before Halls stopped it, and ran after Coke. Halls jumped out, too. He did not even switch off the headlights.

3 All Coke's training as a soldier helped him now. Baxter was just behind him when Coke suddenly turned. Baxter tried to grab him but almost   25
lost his balance. Then Coke hit him on the chin as hard as he could. Baxter fell to the ground heavily. At that moment, Halls jumped on Coke from behind but Coke threw him over his back and against a tree, and then ran back towards the road before Halls could get up. Even when he did, he fell back to the ground again. There was a terrible   30
pain in his ribs. Coke saw the police car very clearly. The headlights were still on, and one of the doors was open. Coke jumped in.
   It took Baxter several seconds to realise where he was. At first, all he could feel was a terrible pain in his jaw. Then he heard the sound of a car engine starting. He looked up and saw Halls pointing to it. Suddenly   35
Baxter realised everything. Halls tried to run after the car but it was too late. Coke was gone and so was their car!

1. Invention Exercise

Ask questions with Are(n't) you, is(n't) he, etc. going to (do).

Example:

PROMPT: Mary/tonight?

RESPONSE: Are you going to see Mary tonight?
   or: Isn't he going to take Mary out
        tonight?
   or: Aren't you going to phone Mary
        tonight?

Prompts:

a) a car/next week   e) married/later
b) the train/soon   f) in England/this summer
c) television/tonight g) that letter/soon
d) a taxi   h) a drink for me

2. Conversation

Two years ago, before he married Susan, Tom taught English in Paris. He taught at an institute for adult students. One evening he went to another institute to give some oral examinations.

TOM: You speak English very well. I'm going to give you a very good mark. Don't worry.

STUDENT (Girl): Thank you very much.

TOM: Not at all. Oh, when you go out, please tell the next student to come in.

STUDENT: Certainly. Good bye (Goes out, closing door. Short pause. Another person comes in).

WOMAN: Excuse me. Are you Mr Atkins?

TOM: Yes. You don't know me, of course. I don't teach here. I just give oral examinations here now and then. Don't be nervous.

WOMAN: Nervous? Who? Me?

TOM: Now, sit down please. I'm going to ask you a few questions. Then we're going to have a short conversation in English. Do you understand?

WOMAN: Yes, of course I do. But may I ask *you* something first?

TOM: After the examination, please. Just concentrate on *my* questions for the moment. First of all, why are you learning English?

WOMAN: Why am I learning English?

TOM: Yes. I mean, what are you going to do with it? Are you going to be a teacher of English, or what?

WOMAN: Please stop just a second. I really *must* ask you something first.

TOM: (irritated) Very well. If you insist.

WOMAN: Would you like a cup of coffee?

TOM: Pardon? What did you say?

WOMAN: You see, I'm English, too. I'm one of the teachers here. I came to ask you if you would like a cup of coffee?

Questions

1. Why did Tom go to the institute that evening?
2. Who did he think the woman was?
3. Who was the woman really?
4. Ask and answer why she came in!

Recall

Without looking at the text, try to remember what Tom and the woman said with these words:

TOM: sit. worry. a few questions. Then/a short conversation. first. why/English? do with it? in your job? a teacher?

WOMAN: stop. something first. teacher here. come/coffee.

e   Summary

Focal points in this Unit.

1. Remember how we use 'going to' to talk about things in the future:

		in a few seconds
a)	They're going to give a party	/in a minute today (=later
b)	We aren't going to watch it	today) this evening
c)	Are you going to tell him?	next week now (very) soon

2. Remember the form of the verb after *if* in sentences like:

'We aren't going to see very much *if she keeps* her hat on.'

'I'm going to get very wet *if the bus doesn't come* soon.'

f Exercises for homework

1. Do all the exercises on pages 51, 52 and 54.

2. Complete these sentences, using 'going to' or 'not going to':

Example:

I watched *Panorama* last week, but . . . (not/next week).

You write:

I watched *Panorama* last week, but I'm not going to watch it next week.

a) Julia caught the 7.45 train yesterday, but . . . (not/tomorrow).
b) I didn't see the film last month, but . . . (next month).
c) She bought some meat in that shop last Monday, but . . . (next time).
d) I didn't travel by air the last time, but . . . (next time).
e) We stayed at home last night, but . . . (not/tonight).

f) I spent £20 on Christmas presents last year, but . . . (not/so much this year).
g) They broadcast the Prime Minister's speech yesterday, and . . . (again tomorrow).
h) We didn't plan our holidays last summer, but . . . (this summer).
i) I visited Bill in hospital this morning, but . . . (not/again today).
j) I didn't pay the bill when it came, but . . . (very soon).

3. **Guided Composition**

Read situation 4 on page 51 again carefully. Then write a telephone conversation between Tom and one of his friends, Bill, which took place a week before the party. Try to use some of the phrases from the Conversation on page 54, too. Begin like this:

TOM: Hello, Bill! This is Tom Atkins here.
BILL: Hello, Tom! How are you?
TOM: Very well, thanks. Look, we're going to give a party next week. Would you like to come?
BILL: Certainly! Who else are you going to invite?

(Note: Use these phrases and words in the conversation: You're not going to . . ., are you?/What time . . .?/20 guests/pop records/ bring anything/plenty to eat and drink/first of all/If you insist.)

4. **Transfer Exercise**

Look at your own diary, agenda or school timetable and write 5 true sentences about things you are going to do tomorrow, the next day or next week.

1

(a) How/Deborah? feel?

(b) What/maid/ say?

(c) What/Deborah/ want?

(d) What/maid?

2

(a) What sort of service/ waiters?

(b) What/Arthur order?

(c) What/ head waiter?

3

(a) What/Tom?

(b) How/last teacher/room

(c) What/student?

(d) Tom saying?

4

(a) When/Peter/ from Canada?

(b) When/plane/ land?

(c) What/Peter/ to customs man?

(d) custom man saying?

5

(a) Who/new boyfriend?

(b) Where/now?

(c) His question?

(d) Julia's answer?

6

(a) What/later?

(b) the men/ask a moment ago?

(c) head waiter saying

1

Deborah feels terrible this morning. "Shall I bring you some tea now?" her maid asked her a few seconds ago. "No, bring me an aspirin instead," Deborah told her. The maid is going to get her the aspirin now.

1. Ask how Deborah feels this morning!
2. What exactly did the maid ask her?
3. What exactly did Deborah tell her?
4. What is the maid going to do?

2

Arthur often eats here. The waiters always give him the best service. The head waiter spoke to Arthur only a minute ago. "Bring me a bottle of your best champagne, please!" Arthur told him. The head waiter is talking to another waiter now. "Take him this champagne!" he is saying. "Take it to him now!"

1. Ask what the waiters always do and why!
2. What did the head waiter do and when?
3. Ask what Arthur told him (and answer)!
4. What is the head waiter saying now?

3

Tom is going to give his class a lesson here, but the last teacher left the room in a terrible mess. A student is going to help him tidy it up. "Would you close the window, please?" Tom is saying. Someone should clean the board and pick the books and chairs up, too.

1. What is Tom going to do?
2. What did the last teacher do?
3. What is that student going to do?
4. What is Tom saying?
5. What else could he say with "Would . . .?"?

4

Tom's younger brother, Peter, flew back from Canada today. His plane landed only a few minutes ago. When the customs officer asked him if he had anything to declare, he told him he hadn't. The customs officer does not believe him. "Would you show me what's in that suitcase?" he is asking.

1. What did Peter do today and when did his plane land?
2. Where is he now?
3. What did the customs officer ask him and what did Peter tell him?
4. What is the customs officer saying now?

5

This is Julia's new boyfriend. He is the one who offered her a lift a few days ago. They are at the cinema now. "Shall I get you some chocolates?" he is asking. "Thank you very much. That's very kind of you," is Julia's answer.

1. Who is the man with Julia and what did he do a few days ago?
2. What is he offering to get her now?
3. What exactly is he saying and what is Julia's answer?

6

There is going to be a party in this room later. A few moments ago, none of the men knew what to do. "Where shall we put the piano?" "What shall I do with the flowers?" they asked. The head waiter is telling them now. "Bring the flowers here and take the piano over there!" he is saying.

1. What is going to happen here later?
2. What questions did the men ask a moment ago and why?
3. What is the head waiter saying now?

FORMATION AND MANIPULATION

1 Pronunciation

Shall is often pronounced [ʃəl] (the weak or unstressed form). Notice the way the teacher says *shall*. Now, read the following sentences aloud until you can say *shall* in its weak form correctly and without hesitation.

  i) Shall I type those letters now?
 ii) When shall I phone you?
iii) Shall I get more flowers?
 iv) Where shall I put the flowers?
  v) What shall I do with the milk?
 vi) Shall I answer the phone for you?

2

A	B	C
Would you	open the door,	please?

  i) What other word can you put in box A to replace 'Would'?
 ii) Look at the situations on page 57; there are many phrases there which you can put in box B.
iii) Now say and/or write ten sentences beginning 'Would/Could you . . .?'

3

A	B	C	D	E
Would you	give	me	a book,	please?

  i) Look at these words: GET   BUY   BRING   SEND
     Which box can you put them in? A, B, or C?
 ii) Think of some other words to replace 'me' in box C.
iii) Now, think of five things which you can put in box D.
 iv) Now write or say some sentences beginning with 'Would/Could you . . .?'

4

A	B	C
Shall I	come in	now?

  i) Look at the situations on page 57. How many words can you find to replace 'come in' in box B?
     Example: 'turn off the light'.
 ii) Here are some more time expressions which you can use in box C:
     SOON   TOMORROW   AT ONCE   IMMEDIATELY
iii) Make questions using the words that can go in boxes A, B and C.

5 Ask the person sitting next to you questions with 'Would/Could you . . .?' and 'Shall I . . .?' using the following prompts:

open the window. show me/him the book. phone me/you later. give me/her a drink of water. switch on the radio. ask them to come in. make me/them a cake. get me/her a newspaper.
The answers to these questions can be:
'Yes, of course' or 'Certainly' or 'I'm sorry but I can't at the moment.'

THE MAN WHO ESCAPED
Episode 10

SYNOPSIS: *When Coke saw Baxter and Halls in a police car, he jumped off his bike and ran into the trees at the side of the road. Baxter and Halls ran after him. Coke managed to get away from both of them and to steal their car.*

1 Coke drove for about twenty minutes. He felt nervous in the police car but he knew it was his only chance.
"I wonder how that policeman managed to contact police-headquarters so quickly?" he asked himself. Then he remembered a newspaper article about the new pocket radios all policemen had. They were small things which they put in their pockets. 5
"Of course! That's it!" he thought. Then he wondered if detectives like Halls and Baxter also had them. He knew they probably did not, because they already had radios in their cars. Suddenly, however, something on the road ahead interrupted his thoughts. Two police cars were there, side by side, blocking the road. Nothing could get by them! 10

2 The two policemen at the road block were bored. It was a lonely spot between two hills and there was very little traffic.
"Could you give me a light, Tom?" one of them said. It was his tenth cigarette that night. Just then, they both looked up and saw a car coming towards them. 15
"It's a police car," the other one said. "Perhaps they're bringing us some hot coffee, or something to eat."
They both watched the car as it came closer. It was a long, straight road and the car was still a good distance away. 20
"Isn't it going to stop?"
"It doesn't look like it."
"Shall we stop it? Our orders are to stop every car."
Just then, they heard the two-tone sound of the horn. It was obvious that whoever was in the car was in a great hurry. 25

3 The two policemen hesitated for a second. Then one of them turned to the other. "Would you move the car out of the way, Bob, or shall I?"
"But our orders were to . . ."
"Look! That's a police car, can't you see? You don't think Coke's going to come through here in a police car, do you?" 30
The other policeman got into the car and moved it back a few inches; the gap was just wide enough for another car to get through now.
"Aren't you going to move back some more?" the other shouted.
Before he could do so, Coke shot through the narrow gap and raced down the road, in the direction of London. 35

1. Invention Exercise

Ask questions with 'Shall I . . .?' or 'Would
you . . .?' using the prompts. Make 2 sentences
from the prompts when you can.

Example:

PROMPT: those books
RESPONSE: Shall I carry those books for you?
      or: Would you carry those books for me?

Prompts:

a) the windows   f) your suitcase
b) that letter   g) the light
c) the grass   h) the radio
d) a cup of tea   i) time
e) your breakfast   j) more clearly/slowly

2. Conversation

Arthur often travels abroad. This is a typical
conversation at the reception desk in a hotel.

RECEPTIONIST: Good evening, sir.
ARTHUR: Good evening. My name's Tigers. I
    believe you have a room reserved for me.
RECEPTIONIST: Just a moment, Mr Tigers. Let's
    see . . . Tigers . . . yes, Mr Tigers, Room 204.
    Would you fill in this form, please?
ARTHUR: Certainly. Er . . . I can't find my pen
    and there isn't one on the desk.
RECEPTIONIST: Isn't there? How strange.
ARTHUR: Perhaps someone walked off with it.
    Could you lend me yours?
RECEPTIONIST: Of course. Here you are. How
    long do you intend to stay, Mr Tigers?
ARTHUR: I'm not sure. It all depends. But I'm
    probably going to leave on Thursday.
RECEPTIONIST: On Thursday. I see. Would you
    tell us as soon as you know?
ARTHUR: Yes, of course. Where shall I put the
    number of my passport?
RECEPTIONIST: Just at the bottom. That's right.
    Thank you.
ARTHUR: Oh, would you wake me up at 7
    tomorrow?

RECEPTIONIST: At 7. Certainly. Porter! Take Mr
    Tigers' suitcase to his room. Just follow the
    porter, Mr Tigers.
ARTHUR: Thank you. Good bye.
RECEPTIONIST: Good bye. Oh! Mr Tigers. My
    pen!
ARTHUR: Your pen?
RECEPTIONIST: Yes. I lent it to you a moment
    ago. You remember?
ARTHUR: Oh yes, of course you did. I put it in
    my pocket by mistake. Here you are. I'm
    very sorry.
RECEPTIONIST: That's quite all right.

Questions

1. What is the first thing Arthur says when he
    goes into the hotel?
2. What is the next thing Arthur has to do?
3. How exactly does the receptionist ask him to
    do this?
4. What does the receptionist do when Arthur
    tells her there isn't a pen on the desk?
5. How does Arthur ask her to do this?
6. What does Arthur say when the receptionist
    asks how long he intends to stay?
7. When does Arthur want to get up and what
    does he say about this?

Correct the statements

1. Arthur lent the receptionist his pen.
2. He is sure he is going to leave on Thursday.
3. Arthur intended to put the pen in his pocket.

Practice

Listen to the tape. Practise the intonation of
'Would you . . .?', Certainly and 'Don't you
remember?'

e   Summary

Focal points in this Unit.

1. Remember the polite way we ask other people to do things for us:

     Would you
     Could you   open the window, please?

2. Remember how we offer to do something:

     Shall I carry that for you?
     Shall I get you some chocolate?

3. With words like *bring, take, get, show, send* and *lend* in the table below use this word order:

1	2	3
Shall I send Could you give	him her them	some tea? the books? the letter?

Notice particularly the form of the words in column 2.

f   Exercises for homework

1. Do all the questions and exercises on pages 57 and 60.

2. Choose the correct form:

   a) Shall I post that letter . . .? (your/you/for you)

   b) Would you send . . . the book, please? (to me/me/I)

   c) Could you lend . . . some money? (him/he/to him)

   d) Shall I take . . . some fruit when I go and see her? (she/to her/her)

   e) Would you give . . . these letters, please? (them/to them/they)

3. Put the words in their correct order to make sentences:

Example:

to give/Tom/a lesson/going/is
Answer: Tom is going to give a lesson.

   a) bring/I/you/a cup of tea/shall?

   b) that phone/you/could/for me/answer?

   c) a light/me/could/give/you?

   d) me/yesterday/sent/a parcel/my parents.

   e) five shillings/them/last night/lent/he.

4. **Guided Composition**

You arrived back from holiday yesterday. Before you went on holiday, you left a book at a friend's house, and you want him (or her) to bring it back as soon as possible. Write a letter asking for it. Begin your letter like this:

     'Dear . . .,
       I flew back from France last night after a wonderful holiday. When I came through the Customs . . .'

Now continue the letter using as many of the following prompt words and phrases as you can, and any other words and phrases from this Unit (particularly pages 57 and 60):

     Customs officer/anything to declare//
     'show/suitcase'//no money/people/offer/
     lift//kind of them//more about holiday/
     see you//remember/book/your house?//
     bring/tomorrow?//

5. **Transfer Exercise**

   a) Write down what you say if you want someone i) to give you a light for your cigarette, ii) to tell you the time, iii) to carry something for you, iv) to answer the phone (or front door), and v) to send you a particular book.

   b) Write down what you say when you offer i) to open a window, ii) to close a door, iii) to help someone, iv) to put something somewhere, and v) to sign a document (hotel register, cheque, letter etc.).

Present perfect with 'For' and 'Since'

1

(a) When/boy friend?

(b) When/Julia?

(c) What time/ now?

(d) Julia/ask?

(e) Why/he/angry?

2

(a) How long/ Tom and Susan?

(b) How long/ house?

(c) How long/the Barclay's?

(d) How long/their house?

3

(a) How long/ Peter/in England?

(b) When/woman?

(c) How long/ Peter/wait?

(d) How long/ woman/talk?

4

(a) How long/ Julia/office?

(b) How long/ others/work?

(c) What/typists?

5

(a) How long/ match?

(b) When/match/ start?

(c) What/police?

(d) What/TV cameras?

(e) Why/Tom/ better view?

HAS/HAVE HAD		10 minutes		9 o'clock	Unit **11**
HAS/HAVE BEEN	FOR	6 months	SINCE	1970	
HAS/HAVE BEEN DOING		3 years		last Friday, etc.	**a**

1

Julia had a date with her new boyfriend in
this restaurant at 8. He came on time but she
did not. She came in only a moment ago. It is 9.
"Have you been waiting long?" she asked him
when she came in. "Yes, I have," he is saying.
He is rather angry because he has been waiting
for an hour.

1. Ask when he came! Ask about Julia, too!
2. What exactly is her question?
3. What exactly is his answer?
4. Why is he angry?

2

Tom and Susan have been married a very short
time. They haven't had that house very long,
either. The couple next door, the Barclays, have
been married a very long time. They have been
living in the same house all that time!

1. Ask questions with 'very long' on the end!
   a) Tom and Susan/married
   b) the Barclays/married
   c) Tom and Susan/that house

3

Tom's brother, Peter, has been back in England
for only half an hour. He is waiting to phone
Tom, but the woman got to the phone box just
a few seconds before he did. That was ten
minutes ago. She has been talking for ten
minutes and Peter has been waiting that long,
too.

1. Ask and answer questions with 'How long'!
   a) Peter/back in England
   b) woman/in the phone box
   c) Peter/outside
   d) talk
   e) wait

4

Julia has not been in the office very long.
Neither have the others. They have been
working for less than ten minutes. They have
been working since 9 o'clock. Actually one
man has just been standing by the window for
the last ten minutes. The two typists have not
been doing very much, either. They have been
talking.

1. Say what each person is doing now!
2. Now ask questions with 'How long'!
3. Make sentences with 'since' and 'for'!

5

This match has been going on for half an hour.
The teams have been playing only since 2.30
and there is trouble already. In the very first
minute, some of the crowd began to throw
things and fight. The police have been trying
to keep order and have been arresting people.
The TV cameras have been filming everything.
There is a very tall man in front of Tom. Tom
has been trying to get a better view for some
time, but it is impossible.

1. Ask and answer questions with 'How long'!
   a) the match   b) the teams
   c) some of the crowd d) the police
   e) the cameras   f) Tom/a better view
2. Make sentences with 'since' and 'for'
   about all the things you see in the picture!

Unit 11
b
FORMATION AND MANIPULATION

1 Pronunciation

a) *I've* is more frequent than *I have* in spoken English, so say *I've* (You've, he's, she's, it's, we've).

b) *for* is almost always pronounced [fə(r)].

2

A	B	C
I've	been living in London	for ages

i) Think of all the other words that can replace 'I've' in box A.

ii) Now look at the situations on page 63 and find words to replace 'been living in London' in box B.

iii) Look at the situations on page 63 again. This time find all the time expressions that can replace 'for ages' in box C.

v) Now, write or say ten sentences using the words that can go in boxes A, B and C.

vi) The word *had* can also go in box B if you put words like 'a car', 'a big house' after it.

vii) Make five sentences with 'I've (etc.) had a . . .'

3

A	B	C	D
How long	has he	been living	in London?

i) Think of all the words which can replace 'has he' in box B.

ii) Now replace boxes C and D (refer to the situations on page 63).

iii) Look at these time expressions, some you know, some are new:

FOR AGES   SINCE LAST SUMMER   FOR A WEEK   SINCE CHRISTMAS   FOR A VERY LONG TIME
SINCE YESTERDAY   FOR YEARS AND YEARS   SINCE 1968   FOR A MOMENT
SINCE HE ARRIVED.

iv) Use the expressions in exercise iii to answer questions beginning with 'How long'. Ask and answer these questions with the person sitting next to you.

Example: A: How long have you been living here?

B: Since last summer.

4

A	B	C
Have you	been in England	very long?

i) Look at these words–they can replace 'been in England' in box B.

'known him'   'had a cold'   'been waiting for them'

ii) With the person sitting next to you, ask and answer 'very long' questions. For positive answers use 'Yes' plus the time expression in Part **3**, exercise iii. For negative answers use the 'No, not very long' or 'No, I haven't' forms.

THE MAN WHO ESCAPED
Episode 11

SYNOPSIS: *Halls and Baxter tried to catch Coke when they saw him on a road in the countryside late at night. Coke, however, got away from them and stole their car. He also got through a police road block.*

1 "How much farther is it to the nearest village?" Baxter asked.
He and Halls were in the middle of the countryside. The night was very dark and there was no traffic on the roads. They could not see a house or even a public phone box anywhere.
"It must be on the other side of that hill" Halls answered.   5
"I hope so! We've been walking for twenty minutes now! When we started, you said it was only ten minutes away!" Baxter said angrily. He was tired and his jaw hurt. He could already imagine the Chief Inspector's comments at their next interview. The Chief Inspector was a very sarcastic man. "Well, Baxter, perhaps you would explain all   10
this to me. It seems you had a car when you saw Coke and that he had it after he saw you. Very interesting. How shall we explain all this to the papers? Shall we say something like 'The police are always ready to help'?"

2 Coke turned off the main road. He wanted to get rid of the police   15
car as soon as possible. The army often used the area for manoeuvres and Coke remembered it from the days when he was a soldier. He knew there was a village down a side road. Just before he got to it, he stopped and left the car in a field. Then he walked into the village itself.
He wanted something and he was sure he could find it here.   20

In his apartment in London, a well-dressed man named Eric Masters turned on the radio and listened. The news was still bad. Coke was still free, the announcer said. Masters looked very frightened. He turned off the radio suddenly and picked up the phone.

3 In a village almost 200 miles away, Coke found what he wanted.   25
"People in villages like this always trust their neighbours. How lucky!" he thought when he saw the motorbike. It was in a garage at the edge of the village. The garage was not even locked and there was a leather motorcycle suit on a nail. There were also a pair of gloves and a helmet. Everyone in the village was asleep. Coke worked silently. He pushed   30
the bike down the road. When he was far enough away from the village he started the engine. It roared loudly. He got on the motorbike and raced towards London.

1. Conversation
for Paired Practice

Read the Model conversation, and use the prompts to make others like it.

MODEL: A: Are you still living in London?
        B: Yes, I've been living there for 3 years now.

Prompts:

1) A: working for them
   B: two years
2) A: those French cigarettes
   B: a couple of months
3) A: studying English
   B: eighteen months
4) A: reading that book
   B: 6 weeks
5) A: writing that letter
   B: half an hour
6) A: waiting to see the boss
   B: ages

2. Conversation

Two months ago Julia bought a pullover from a large department store. The pullover is worn out already. Julia took the pullover back during the lunch hour today. She went there with a friend, Mary, who works in the same office. This is what happened.

MARY: It's certainly very busy here today, isn't it?

JULIA: Yes, and there aren't enough salesgirls. We've been standing here for at least five minutes!

MARY: Quick. Catch that salesgirl's eye! She's just finishing with a customer.

JULIA: Miss! Miss! Excuse me. I think I'm next and I haven't very much time.

SALESGIRL: Yes, madam. How can I help you?

JULIA: I'm afraid I have a complaint. It's this pullover. I've only had it for two months and it's already worn out.

SALESGIRL: Worn out? May I see it?

JULIA: Yes, here you are. Look at the sleeves. They're the worst part. Do you see? They've worn very badly.

SALESGIRL: And how long do you say you've had it?

JULIA: For only two months. Since Christmas, in fact. Look, here's the receipt.

SALESGIRL: Thank you. This is very strange. We've been selling this particular make for years and we haven't had any complaints in all that time.

JULIA: Well, I'm sorry. I'm sure it isn't my fault it's already worn out.

SALESGIRL: One moment, please. Let me call the manager. Mr Simons! Mr Simons!

MR SIMONS: Yes?

SALESGIRL: It's this lady. She's had this pullover for two months and it's already worn out.

MR SIMONS: Really? Let me see, please. Hmmm . . . yes . . .

JULIA: I've been wearing it at the week-ends; that's all.

MR SIMONS: Yes, well . . . make out a credit-slip for the lady, would you, Miss Smith?

JULIA: A credit-slip?

MR SIMONS: Yes. You can buy anything you like with it in the store.

JULIA: I'd rather have my money back, if you don't mind.

MR SIMONS: I see. Well, I suppose we can arrange that.

JULIA: Thank you.

Correct the statements

1. There are not many people in the shop today.
2. Julia has a lot of time.
3. She has been standing there for an hour.
4. She has had the sweater for a year.
5. The shop hasn't been selling that particular make for long.
6. Julia has been wearing the sweater at work.
7. Julia wants a credit-slip for the sweater.

Answer these questions

1. Ask and answer how long Julia has been standing there!
2. Ask why!
3. Why is she not satisfied with the pullover?
4. What exactly does she say when the manager offers her a credit-slip?

Practice

Think of some more sentences of your own using the pattern 'I'd rather . . ., if you don't mind'. Describe the situations we can use these sentences in.

e   Summary

Focal points in this Unit.

1. a) Look at the ideas which are expressed in a 'have been' sentence:

   I am in London. | I have been in
   I came here 3 | London for
   years ago. | 3 years.

   b) Now look at a 'have had' sentence:

   I have a car. |
   I bought it 6 | I have had a car
   months ago. | for 6 months.

   c) Now look at a 'have been (do)ing' sentence:

   It is snowing. |
   It started snowing | It has been snow-
   an hour ago. | ing for an hour.

2. To ask questions about a period of time we use the form:

   How long   +   have been doing . . .?
                  have had . . .?

   Example:

   How long have you been learning French?
   How long have you had that hat?

3. Remember that *since* is used with times that we can point to on a calendar or clock.

                 6 o'clock/yesterday/
   since   +   last Monday/last January/
                 15th March/1966/Easter

   since is also used with phrases to which the speaker can put a definite time or date.

                 the end of the war/I was 6/
                 I left school/she got married/
   since   +   his last birthday/
                 the last office party

4. Remember that *for* is used with periods of time.

                 half an hour/45 minutes/
                 3 hours/2 days/6 weeks/
   for   +   a fortnight/18 months/
                 25 years/ages and ages/
                 a week or so

f   Exercises for homework

1. Do all the exercises and questions on pages 63, 64 and 66.

2. **Invention Exercise**

   With 'has/have been doing . . . for/since'

   Examples:

   a) PROMPT: work/Bristol/2 years.
      RESPONSE: I've been working in Bristol for 2 years.
   b) PROMPT: live/London/1965.
      RESPONSE: She's been living in London since 1965.

   Prompts:

   a) wait/bus/10 minutes
   b) learn/English/6 months
   c) work/garden/1 o'clock
   d) smoke/heavily/2 years
   e) drive/that car/3 years
   f) live/a flat/last July
   g) build/that house/March
   h) look for/prisoner/he escaped
   i) ring/bell/5 minutes

3. **Guided Composition**

   Write a letter of complaint to a shop about a woollen pullover you bought while you were on holiday in England about a month ago. You want to complain because it has worn very badly. Read the Conversation on page 66 again, and try and use as many of the words, phrases and patterns as you can in your letter: these patterns are particularly useful – 'I'm afraid I have a complaint'/'. . . it's already worn badly'/'it isn't my fault . . .'/'I'd rather . . ., if you don't mind.' Begin your letter like this:

   'Dear Sir,
       While I was on holiday in your town about a month ago, I bought a green pullover in your shop. I'm afraid . . .'

4. **Transfer Exercise**

   Write 10 true sentences about yourself or friends using 'have done', 'have been' or 'have been doing' + *since* or *for*:
   For example: 'I've had this car for 3 years'/ 'I've been learning English since 1969'.

Have been doing/have just done/ haven't done yet/had better do

1

(a) How long/ they/club?

(b) What time?

(c) good time?

(d) What/Deborah/ say?

(e) Where/other people?

2

(a) Fred/good time?

(b) Where/his wife?

(c) Why/quiet?

3

(a) Where/Julia?

(b) How long/ bus?

(c) What/round corner?

4

(a) What/Peter?

(b) How long?

(c) What/operator?

(d) Why/Peter/ hang up?

5

(a) Who/Peter/ stay with?

(b) How long/ job?

(c) What/Tom/ tell/Peter?

6

(a) How/Frank/ lately?

(b) Why/overtime?

(c) What/doctor/ say?

1

Arthur and Deborah have been in a night-club since 8 p.m. It is 2 in the morning now. They have been having a very good time. "I really think we had better leave now" Deborah is telling Arthur. "Everybody else has gone home except the waiter and the band."

1. Ask and answer the questions!
   a) Where/now   b) How long
   c) What time/now   d) a good time
2. What is Deborah telling Arthur?
3. Do you agree? Why?

2

Fred Collins has been having a good time, too. He has just come home. His wife is asleep upstairs. He had better be very quiet. He had better look where he is going. His wife is going to be very angry if he wakes her up.

1. What has Fred been doing?
2. What has he just done?
3. What is going to happen if he is not careful?
4. Make some sentences about him with 'had better' and 'had better not'!

3

Julia is going to meet her boyfriend. She has been waiting for the bus for some time but it has not come yet. She is going to be late again if it does not come soon. A taxi has just come round the corner. Perhaps she had better take it.

1. What is Julia going to do?
2. What is she doing now? Ask 'how long'!
3. What is going to happen if the bus does not come soon?
4. What has just happened?
5. What had she better do?

4

Peter is making a long-distance call to Canada. He has been talking for six minutes and the operator has just asked him to put some more money in. He has not got any. "Look," he is saying to the person in Canada, "I think I'd better hang up now."

1. What is Peter doing?
2. Ask how long (and answer)!
3. What has the operator just asked him to do?
4. What is he saying?

5

Peter came back to England a month ago. He has been staying with Tom and Susan since then. He has been looking for a job for a month but has not found one yet. "Some employers don't like people with long hair," Tom is telling him. "Perhaps you'd better get a haircut!"

1. Ask and answer questions about Peter!
   a) When/back to England
   b) How long/with Tom and Susan
   c) How long/a job
   d) one yet
2. What is Tom telling him?

6

Frank Martin has not been feeling very well lately. He has been working a lot of overtime because he wants to buy a new car. The doctor has been examining him. "You've been working too hard, that's all," he is saying. "You'd better take things easy for a while. You'd better not work so hard."

1. What has the doctor been doing?
2. What had Frank better do and why?
3. Ask and answer the questions!
   a) very well lately
   b) Why/so much overtime lately

Unit 12
b

FORMATION AND MANIPULATION

1

A	B	C
He's been	having a good time	

i) Find other words to replace 'He's been' in box A.

ii) Look at the situations on page 69 and find things to put in box B.

iii) Box C is empty. Words like *recently* and *lately* can go here, so can expressions of time with the words *since* and *for*. Think of as many as you can. If you can't think of many, look at the Formation and Manipulation page of Unit 11.

iv) With the person sitting next to you, ask and answer questions like this:
Question: What's he been doing recently?
Answer: Having a good time, *or* He's been having a good time.

v) Now make questions starting 'Have you . . .?' (answer, 'Yes, I have' or 'No, I haven't').
Example: Question: Have you been having a good time recently?
    Answer: Yes, I have.

---

2 Look at these words: LOOKING   FEELING   EATING
i) Now look at the first sentence of situation 6, page 69.

ii) Find other words to replace 'Frank Martin', 'feeling' and 'lately'.

iii) With the person sitting next to you, ask and answer questions like this:
Question: What's the matter with Frank Martin?
Answer: Oh, he hasn't been feeling very well lately.
and like this:
Question: What's the matter?
Answer: Well, actually, I haven't been feeling very well lately.

3

A	B	C	D	E
Has he	come in	yet?	Yes, he's just	come in

i) Think of words to replace 'he' in boxes A and D.

ii) Now, think of words to replace 'come in' in boxes B and E.

iii) Now say or write five sentences using the new words you have.

---

4 i) Make sentences from the table.

You'd better	get a meal
We'd better	go now
I'd better	find a taxi

ii) Make sentences from the table.

You'd better not	work so hard
He'd better not	eat so much
They'd better not	smoke so much

NOTE: 'We'd' is the short form of 'We had' but we always say and write *'d*. For example: 'You'd better get a haircut' Page 69, situation 5.

SYNOPSIS: *Coke knew it was dangerous to stay in the police car, so he stole a motorbike from a small village.*

1 Eric Masters had the face of a man who lived comfortably and ate well. It was the face of a man who usually did not worry about the future. All this was gone now. He was very worried indeed when he picked up the phone and dialled nervously. At first, nobody answered at the other end. The phone rang at least twelve times but Masters did not hang   5 up. Finally a sleepy voice answered angrily, "Who is it? What the devil do you want at this hour?"
It was a man's voice, and it was educated and smooth, but it had a cruel, cold edge.

2 "Is that you, Hugo? This is Eric," Masters said quickly.   10
The man at the other end became even angrier.
"And why are you ringing at this hour? I've been in bed for an hour!"
"But, haven't you heard the news, Hugo? Coke's still free!"
"Of course I've heard. So have my friends," the man answered coldly.
"I can't sleep. I've been thinking about Coke all evening!"   15
"Perhaps you'd better take a sleeping pill!"
Masters almost screamed the next question into the phone. "What are you going to do, Hugo? What are you going to do?"
The man at the other end answered just as coldly and as calmly as before, "Do? We're going to kill Coke! That's what we're going to do.   20
That is, if he is stupid enough to come to London!"

3 The motorbike was fast but the roads were icy. Coke drove dangerously. He knew he had to. He had very little time.
"I'd better keep to the side roads," he thought, but he did not because the main road was much faster, and he had very little time. A police   25
car went by in the opposite direction. He began to feel a little safer. Then, around 2 o'clock in the morning, he suddenly saw lights in his mirror. They were the headlights of another police car, and this time it was just behind him. It came closer and closer and then suddenly speeded up. For several seconds, Coke and the car raced along side by   30
side. Coke looked up. The two policemen in the car were looking at him but they could not see his face clearly. He was wearing a helmet and goggles. Coke raised his hand and waved casually. The driver was already looking at the road again, but the other still had his eyes on Coke. Then, the car speeded up again. In a few seconds it was far   35
ahead of him. Coke raced towards London. He knew exactly where he wanted to go.

1. Invention Exercise

Make sentences with 'had better do' using the prompts.

Examples:

1) PROMPT: those shoes.
   RESPONSE: You'd (He'd/I'd, etc.) better clean those shoes.
2) PROMPT: up early tomorrow
   RESPONSE: I'd better get up early tomorrow.

Prompts:

a) a haircut
b) very quiet
c) that old car
d) the bank
e) less beer
f) bed early tonight
g) that letter now
h) a new car
i) the office earlier
j) more slowly
k) faster
l) a phone call

Describe the situations in which the sentences are used.

2. Conversation

Frank Martin went to see his doctor last week, but he was not satisfied with what the doctor told him. He asked to see a specialist. Like everybody else in Great Britain, Frank can insist on this. He does not have to pay for this or any other medical treatment. This is what happened when he saw Dr Scott, the specialist.

DR SCOTT: Now, Mr Martin. I've just been reading what your own doctor says. I gather you haven't been feeling very well lately? Is that right?

FRANK: It's . . . it's my leg, doctor. My right leg. I keep getting a strange pain in it.

DR SCOTT: Could you describe this pain to me?

FRANK: It's like . . . like boiling water running down my leg. It's been getting worse lately, too. I've been losing sleep.

DR SCOTT: You mean the pain's been keeping you awake?

FRANK: Yes, that's right. It's been keeping me awake.

DR SCOTT: Now, tell me, how long have you had this trouble?

FRANK: The pain? For about a year now.

DR SCOTT: Hmmm . . . Have you been getting tired lately after you've been for a walk? For instance, have you been getting a bit short of breath, perhaps?

FRANK: Why, yes! Yes, I have, doctor!

DR SCOTT: Hmmm . . . I think we'd better give you a few tests here in hospital.

FRANK: Do you think it's serious, doctor?

DR SCOTT: Probably not.

FRANK: But . . . Doctor Cooke, my local doctor, thinks it's only that I've been working too hard lately.

DR SCOTT: That could be the reason. Don't worry. We'll soon find out.

Correct the statements

1. Frank has been getting a strange pain in his arm.
2. It has been getting better lately.
3. Frank's own doctor thinks he has been eating too much lately.
4. The specialist thinks what the other doctor says is impossible.

Questions

1. What has the pain been doing to Frank?
2. What has been happening to Frank after he has been for a walk?
3. What does the specialist think they had better do?

Ask and answer the questions about Frank

1. How long/this trouble?
2. pain/better or worse lately?

e Summary

Focal points in this Unit.

1. Remember how we use the words *just* and *yet* with the Present Perfect Simple:
   a) 'He has *just* come home'. 'A taxi has *just* come round the corner'. '. . . the operator has *just* asked him to put some more money in'.
   b) 'The bus has not come *yet*'. 'He has not found a job *yet*'.
   Notice particularly where we put them in a sentence.

2. Remember how we use 'had better' to give advice to other people–'You *had better not work* so hard'.–and to suggest that it is a good idea to do something–'We *had better leave* now'./'I *had better not* tell them'. Notice particularly the form of the verb after 'had better', and the position of *not* in a negative sentence.

f Exercises for homework

1. Do all the questions and exercises on pages 69 and 72.

2. **Invention Exercise**

   Write sentences using the prompts:

   MODEL: I've been . . . $\begin{array}{c}\text{for}\\\text{since}\end{array}$ . . ., but I haven't . . . yet.

   Examples:

   a) PROMPT: job/three weeks
      RESPONSE: I've been looking for a job for three weeks, but I haven't found one yet.
   b) PROMPT: the bus/9 o'clock
      RESPONSE: I've been waiting for the bus since 9 o'clock, but it hasn't come yet.
   a) my homework/half an hour
   b) the train/twenty minutes
   c) the concert/7.30

d) a car/20 years
e) the postman/8 o'clock
f) this book/2 weeks
g) English/18 months
h) this letter/6 o'clock
i) a sports car/last Christmas
j) pop records/20 minutes

3. **Guided Composition**

   Using some of the vocabulary and sentence patterns from situation 6 (page 69) and from the Conversation (page 72), write a short letter to a friend politely refusing an invitation to go on a long walk in the country. Begin your letter like this:

   'Dear . . .,
      Thank you very much for your invitation to go on a long walk next week-end. It was very nice of you to think of me, but I'm afraid . . .'

4. **Transfer Exercise**

   Write at least 5 sentences about yourself using this pattern:

   I haven't done the job yet, so I'd better do it as soon as I can.
   I haven't booked the tickets for the concert yet, so I'd better book them this afternoon.

Past continuous and past simple

1

(a) What/people/doing?

(b) first time?

(c) What/director?

(d) What/all the different people?

(e) When/'cut'/last time?

(f) What/the different people/then?

2

(a) What/all the people/Charles jumped?
(ask two questions about each person)

3

(a) What/in a few seconds?

(b) What/Frank/now?

(c) some of the men?

(d) old man?

(e) manager?

(f) What/manager/bell rings?

4

(a) What/old lady?

(b) What/two old men?

(c) What/young man?

(d) What/children?

(e) What/young couple?

He/she	WAS DOING	
We/you/they	WERE DOING	. . . . when . . . . DID
He (etc.)	DID	

Unit 13

a

1

These people are making a film. This is the second time they have filmed this scene. The director is going to shout "cut" in a second. Two men are fighting. The King is talking to the Queen. She is listening. A beautiful girl is crying. Two other men are watching the fight. One of them is laughing. The director shouted "cut" at exactly this point before. They were all doing the same thing when he did this. They all stopped and had a short rest when he shouted "cut".

1. Ask what these people are doing now and answer:
   a) the two men   b) the King
   c) the Queen   d) the beautiful girl
   e) the two other men
2. Now say what all these people were doing when the director shouted "cut" at this point before. Make at least five different sentences!
3. What did they all do when the director shouted "cut" last time? (short rest)

3

This is where Frank works. You can see exactly the same thing every day at this time. A bell is going to ring in a few seconds and everybody is going to rush out, as they always do. Frank is working at his machine. Some of the men are watching the clock. An old man is sweeping the floor and the factory manager is standing in front of his office. He is looking at his watch and at the men. He always goes back into his office when the bell rings. This is exactly what was happening when the bell rang yesterday, too.

1. Notice the question "Was Frank working when the bell rang yesterday?"
   Notice the short answer using the same model: "Yes, he was"/"No, he wasn't"!
   a) Frank/the clock?
   b) manager/his watch?
   c) old man/the floor?
   d) some of the men/clock? etc.
2. Now ask what these people did when the bell rang (and answer)!

2

This is a scene from one of Charles Kay's very old films. It was called "Terror in the Castle". Charles played a monster, half-man, half-gorilla. Everybody was having dinner when he jumped down. A girl was playing the lyre. The King was drinking wine. The Queen was laughing and the King's brother was smiling at her. The King's son was kissing one of the Queen's maids. A second later, the monster jumped down and they all ran away.

1. Ask what each person was doing in this old film when Charles jumped down. Give full answers! Then say what each person did when he jumped down!

4

These two pictures show both what was happening and what happened in a park yesterday when it suddenly began to rain. An old lady was feeding some pigeons. Two old men were sitting on a park bench and talking. A young man was looking at the flowers. A young couple were walking hand in hand. Some children were playing on the swings. When it began to rain the two old men got up and stood under a tree. The old woman put a newspaper over her head and the young man put his umbrella up. The young couple and the children began to run as fast as they could.

1. What do these two pictures show? What happened suddenly?
2. Ask questions about these people with "What was/were . . . ing when it began to rain?"
3. Now ask "What did . . . do when it began to rain?"

Unit 13
b

FORMATION AND MANIPULATION

---

1 Pronunciation

was and *were* are words that have weak or unstressed forms which are used very frequently in spoken English.

We write: *I was there*   and *We were there*.

BUT WE SAY: I [wəz] there and We [wə] there.

2

A	B	C	D	E
She	was working	when	he	arrived

i) Think of other words to replace 'she' and 'he' in boxes A and D. Don't forget that you can also use names in these boxes.

ii) Read the situation on page 75 again and look for verbs to replace 'work' and 'arrive' in boxes B and E.

iii) Now write or say ten sentences using the new words you have for the boxes.

iv) Here are some more words which you can use to make sentences like 'She was working when he arrived.'

B	D and E
eating breakfast having a bath doing the washing-up writing a letter making tea watching television washing the children	the phone rang. Joe arrived. the light went out. someone knocked at the door. the man left. the clock stopped. the news started. the house caught fire. the baby was sick.

v) Now, with the words in the boxes in exercise iv, ask and answer questions like this:
Question: What were you doing when the phone rang?
Answer: (I was) watching television.

3

A	B	C	D	E
I	stood up	when	Bill	came in.

i) Look at situations 2 and 4 on page 75, you will find many verbs to replace those in boxes B and E.

ii) Use those and these below to make ten new sentences like: 'I stood up when Bill came in.'

B	E
stood up stopped talking went away sat down opened the door smiled	Bill came in. the policeman left. the film-star came in. the music stopped.

iii) Now, with the person sitting next to you, ask questions using the items in box E and answer them with the items in box B:
Example: Question: What did you do when the policeman left?
Answer: (I) sat down.

THE MAN WHO ESCAPED
Episode 13

SYNOPSIS: *Eric Masters, a man who knew Coke before Coke went to prison, phoned a man called Hugo. Masters was terribly worried. For some reason, he was very afraid of Coke.*

1 Coke reached London just before 6. The huge city was just beginning to wake up but the streets were still dark. He drove to a block of small flats not far from the river in the south east. There was a light on in one of the ground floor flats. It was shining in the kitchen. He went to the window and tapped softly. He was still standing at the window   5 when the back door opened. When he looked up, a woman was standing there. He hesitated when he saw her and almost went back into the shadows again, but she looked at him calmly. "Come in, Ted. I've been expecting you," she said very softly. He walked towards her and stood in the open doorway.   10
"I haven't got any right to ask for your help," he said after a pause.
"But there's nobody else you can go to, is there? You'd better come in," she answered calmly.

2 Baxter caught a very early train to London. When he got to Scotland Yard, the Chief Inspector was waiting for him. When Baxter went into   15 his office, he was sitting at his desk and looking at a photograph. The Inspector looked at Baxter quickly, then back at the photo. "Perhaps it was a good thing you didn't catch Coke after all," he said suddenly. Baxter stared at him in surprise.
"What do you mean, sir? I don't understand."   20
"I have a picture here of a man who knew Coke in the army. He was also a witness at Coke's trial. I've been interested in the man for some time now. Perhaps we'll be able to find out more about him now that Coke's free," the Inspector said, and gave Baxter the photograph.
"This is the man. Watch him. Follow him everywhere!"   25
Baxter looked at the man in the photo carefully. It was Eric Masters.

3 "You really shouldn't help me, Kate. It's against the law," Coke said. He and the young woman were sitting in her kitchen. He was eating breakfast hungrily. Kate did not say anything.
"I mean, everybody thinks I'm a spy," he went on.   30
"But I don't think so," she finally said. Coke finished his breakfast silently. Then he said, "You were the only person who ever believed I was innocent. That's why I came to you. Who else will help me?"
"Help you to do what, Ted?" Kate asked.
"Help me to find the real spies," he answered slowly.   35

Unit **13**
d

1. Practice Situations

Make 2 sentences for each of these situations, one with 'was doing . . . when . . . did' and one with 'did . . . when . . . did'.

Example Situation:

Robert drove to Southampton yesterday. Halfway there the car broke down. Robert walked to a garage to get a mechanic.

Example Sentences:

1) Robert *was driving* to Southampton yesterday *when* his car *broke down*.
2) *When* his car *broke down*, Robert *walked* to a garage to get a mechanic.

Situations:

a) Julia watched television last night. The phone rang in the middle of the programme. She answered it.
b) Arthur played golf yesterday afternoon. Halfway round the course he received a telegram. He left immediately.
c) Deborah went to the cinema yesterday afternoon. During the performance the film broke down. She then went home.
d) The policeman walked down the High Street yesterday morning. A man asked him the time. The policeman told him.

2. Conversation

Tom Atkins saw an accident between two cars last month. He is a witness in court today. You are going to hear the lawyer for one of the drivers, then Tom, and then the lawyer for the other driver.

1ST LAWYER: Mr Atkins, would you please tell the court what you were doing when the accident happened and what you saw?
TOM: Yes, I was driving home from work. It was about 5.15, and there was a blue car in front of me. We were both driving along Harbour Road when a small white Ford suddenly shot out of a side road. It shot right in front of the blue car. The driver tried to stop, but it was impossible. He ran into the white Ford.
1ST LAWYER: I see. Now, how fast was the car in front of you going when the accident happened?

TOM: The blue car? 30 miles an hour. Certainly no more than that.
1ST LAWYER: And the white Ford shot out without any warning?
TOM: Yes, that's right.
1ST LAWYER: Thank you, Mr Atkins.
2ND LAWYER: Mr Atkins! How can you be sure the blue car was only doing 30?
TOM: Because I was only doing 30, and the blue car wasn't going any faster than I was.
2ND LAWYER: Are you sure of that? Absolutely positive?
TOM: Yes, I am. I'm positive!
2ND LAWYER: Positive? How can you be so positive, Mr Atkins? Were you looking at your speedometer when the accident happened?
TOM: Of course not. I was looking at the road ahead. That's how I managed to see the accident!
2ND LAWYER: Well, if you weren't looking at your speedometer how can you possibly be sure how fast you were going?
TOM: Because I never go faster than 30 on that road. It's against the law, that's why!

Correct the statements

1. Tom was driving in front of the blue car.
2. The white Ford shot right in front of him.
3. The blue car was doing about 50 miles an hour.
4. The blue car was going faster than Tom was.
5. Tom was looking at the speedometer when the accident happened.

Questions

1. Whose fault do you think the accident was? Say why?
2. Do you think the blue car was driving dangerously at all? Give reasons.
3. Ask and answer these questions about Tom when the accident happened:
   a) how fast?   c) from work or to work?
   b) looking at?
4. How does Tom know what speed he was doing when the accident happened?
5. Who do you think the first lawyer is defending? Who do you think the second lawyer is defending? Give reasons!

e   Summary

Focal points in this Unit.

1. Note the formation of the Past Continuous Tense:
   a) I, he, she, it was/we, you they were + doing.
   b) Questions and negatives are formed like this:

   He wasn't/we weren't doing . . .
   Was he/were they doing . . .?

2. Remember that there is an important difference between two sentences like this:
   He was crossing the road when he saw me.
   and this:
   He stopped when he saw me.
   In these sentences, 'he was crossing' is a background idea, 'he stopped' is a simple action.

f   Exercises for homework

1. Do all the exercises and questions on pages 75 and 78.

2. Invention Exercise

Example:

PROMPTS: to work this morning/an accident
RESPONSE: I was walking to work this morning when I saw an accident.
or: John was riding to work this morning when he had an accident.

Prompts:

a) breakfast/the telephone
b) lesson/bell
c) my shirt/a button (off)
d) along the road/a banana skin
e) the guitar/a string
f) newspaper/bus
g) in the park/a friend
h) tennis/rain
i) homework/noise outside

3. Complete these sentences (using 'was/were doing' or 'did')–i.e. past simple
   a) I was walking through the park yesterday when . . .
   b) When I opened the door . . .
   c) It was snowing when . . .
   d) I was ringing the doorbell when . . .
   e) When I got to the lesson, . . .

4. Guided Composition

Read situations 1 and 2 on page 75 again very carefully. Then write about a short visit to a film studio. Begin like this
   'The other day I went to visit a film studio. When I got there, a friend met me, and we went straight to where they were shooting a scene for . . .'.
Say what sort of film they were making, and describe what the different people were doing when you got there. Describe, too, what they all did when they stopped for the lunch break. Finally, describe what some of the people were doing when you left later in the afternoon.

5. Transfer Exercise

Write 5 sentences about yourself which are true. Use the tenses we have practised in this Unit.
If you write this as an example: *I was driving to London last week-end when my car broke down.*
then add another sentence, perhaps: *When my car broke down, I phoned a garage.*
Or if you write this as an example: *I got out of bed this morning when my alarm rang.*
then add another sentence, perhaps: *I was sleeping when my alarm-clock began to ring.*
or: *When I got out of bed, the sun was shining through the window.*

The simple future used in requests, offers, and of 'Must' and 'Can'

1

(a) When/Fred/army?

(b) What/doctor/going to do?

(c) Fred ask?

(d) doctor answer?

2

(a) What/Susan ask Tom?

(b) Where/Peter?

(c) What/Peter/say?

3

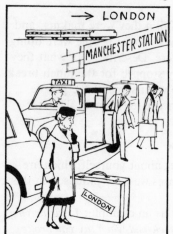

(a) What can't/old lady?

(b) What must/do?

(c) Where/to?

(d) What/there?

4

(a) What/Tom a moment ago?

(b) How/offer?

(c) How/old lady/thank him?

5

(a) What/Tom doing?

(b) What/Peter/say?

(c) serious?

6

(a) How/Frank?

(b) What/doctor/say?
(for a week)
(every six hours)

(c) What/Frank/tomorrow?

"WILL YOU . . . . ?" in requests/"I'LL" used in offers of help
Future of MUST and CAN
Reflexive Pronouns used emphatically as in "I can't do this myself"

Unit **14**

a

1

Fred Collins joined the army a few days ago.
A doctor is going to give him an injection in the
arm.

"Will it hurt?" Fred wants to know.
"No, don't worry. It won't hurt at all.
You won't even feel it," the doctor is saying.

1. What is the doctor going to do?
2. What exactly is Fred's question?
3. What is the exact answer?
4. Ask the questions with 'Will'. Give short
   answers with 'Yes, it/he will' or 'No, it/he
   won't'
   a) hurt   b) Fred feel it
   c) be very pleasant

2

Susan wrote a letter and asked Tom to post it
only a second ago. She said "Will you post this
for me, Tom? It must catch the next post."

Peter is going out for a walk. "I'll post it
for you. I'm going out for a walk anyway," he
is saying.

1. What did Susan ask Tom to do a second ago?
2. How exactly did she ask him to do this?
3. Why has Peter got his coat on?
4. What is he saying?

3

The old lady cannot carry her case herself.
"I can't possibly carry this myself. I must
find a porter!" she is thinking. She is in
Manchester now. She is going to catch a train
to London. She will have to find a porter there,
too. She won't be able to carry that case then,
either.

1. Where is the old lady now?
2. What must she do now and why?
3. Where is she going?
4. What will she have to do there and why?

4

Tom is going to catch the same train. He
noticed the old lady a moment ago and offered
to help.

"I'll carry that case for you. You can't
possibly carry it yourself," he said. The old
lady is thanking him. "Thank you. That's
very kind of you."

1. When did Tom notice her and what did he
   offer to do?
2. What exactly did he say?
3. What is the old lady doing now?
4. What exactly is she saying?

5

Tom is looking at the engine of his car. There
is something wrong with it and he does not
think he can possibly repair it himself. "I'll
help you. Perhaps we can do it ourselves!"
Peter is saying. Actually it is something very
serious. Tom and Peter cannot possibly repair
it themselves. They will have to get a mechanic.

1. What is Tom looking at and why?
2. Ask and answer the questions
   a) Tom/repair it himself
   b) Peter think/themselves
3. What exactly is Peter saying?
4. What will they have to do and why?

6

Frank Martin is very ill. The doctor is talking
to him.

"You'll have to stay in bed for a week and
you'll have to take this medicine every six
hours."

Frank has a ticket for a big football match
tomorrow. He won't be able to use it.

1. Why is the doctor there?
2. Ask questions about Frank with "Will he
   have to . . .?" or "Will he be able to . . .?"
   Answer "Yes, he will" or "No, he won't"!
   a) in bed very long
   b) medicine very often
   c) that ticket
   d) the match tomorrow
   e) on television

1 Use this table to ask someone else to do something for you. Imitate Susan's intonation in situation 2.

Will you	post this letter carry this bag give Mr. Kent this message play that record sing that song again	for	them her me him us	?

2 With another person, make a conversation using this table. Imitate Tom's intonation in situation 4.

A:	I'll	carry that bag answer the phone do the dishes post the letter close the window	for you.	B:	Thank you.	That's very	nice kind good helpful	of you!

3 How many sentences can you make from this table? Make at least twelve orally.

You	will/won't	have to be able to	work late see the boss go to that film take the test post the letter	tomorrow some other time later next week

Notice the question forms and the short answers

Will you	be able to have to	come again?

Yes, I will/No, I won't.

Ask someone else questions with these prompts:
(Tell that person to give short answers.)

see me this evening. play golf tomorrow.
work late this evening. give me an answer soon.
repair the car yourself. take it to a mechanic.

4 i) Look at and repeat these words aloud: myself himself herself itself yourself
ourse*lves* yourse*lves* themse*lves*

ii) Now make sentences with those words and
these prompts:
Example: little girl/that heavy bag. (That little
girl cannot carry that heavy bag herself.)
    1. little girl/all that ice-cream
    2. We/all this work

3. Tom and Peter/all that work
4. Susan/all the dirty dishes
5. Arthur/all that champagne
6. I/this difficult question
7. We/all these books
8. Tom/that broken chair

iii) Notice that when we are speaking directly to *more than one person,* we use 'yourse*lves*'.
Example: 'All right, children. You'll have to clean up the room yourselves!'

THE MAN WHO ESCAPED
Episode 14

SYNOPSIS: *(Note: The synopsis now uses all tenses previously introduced)*
Baxter caught the train back to London early this morning. He is now in the Chief Inspector's office. The Chief Inspector has just told him to follow Masters everywhere. Meanwhile, Coke is hiding in Kate's flat.

1 Kate was what the Americans call 'a cool character'; nothing seemed to surprise her very much. She seemed ready for anything. Perhaps this was because she was an actress. She played small parts in films and on television. Her life was full of surprises. Just then she was not working at all. Perhaps that was why she did not hesitate even for a 5 second when Coke said he wanted her help to find the real spies.
"All right," she said. "I'll help you and I'll start right now. Wait here!"
"What do you mean? Where are you going?" Coke asked.
"You'll find out when I come back. I'll have to get some things now!"
Before Coke could ask her anything more, she was gone. 10

2 Not very far away, Baxter was still sitting in the Chief Inspector's Office. He was still looking at Masters' photograph. He looked up.
"What's so interesting about him? Why do you want me to follow him?" he asked.
"A few days ago, quite by accident we learned a few things about him. 15 Coke might . . . notice I say 'might' . . . be innocent after all. It's only a possibility. We want to see what Masters does if Coke contacts him," the Chief Inspector answered. Baxter was even more surprised now.
"I don't understand, sir? What do you think Masters might do?" he said. 20
"Masters might try to kill him if he's really afraid of him."
"But surely that's dangerous, sir. I mean, if Coke is innocent, Masters might kill him . . . and if he isn't innocent, we're letting him go free. After all, Coke might kill Masters . . . or someone else!"
The Chief Inspector looked very serious. 25
"That's a chance we'll have to take, Baxter!" he said.

3 Time passed very slowly for Coke that morning and afternoon. He slept a bit but then got up and walked about the flat nervously. It was evening before Kate came back. The winter sun was just setting when she came through the door. She was carrying a large bundle and a lot 30 of other things.
"Where have you been? You've been gone for hours!" he said.
"Yes, I've been busy. Here. Try these things on," she answered. She unwrapped the bundle quickly and showed him a suit, shoes and shirt. There was also a coat with an expensive fur collar, the sort millionaires 35 wear in films. Coke put the clothes on unwillingly. "I'll have to change my appearance more than this!" he said.
"Of course you will," she answered. "And I've got just the things you'll need!"

Unit 14
d

1. Practice Situations

Make 2 sentences for each situation, one with 'He'll/she'll/they'll have to . . .' and one with 'He/she/they won't be able to . . .'

Example Situation:

Julia usually catches the 8.15 bus. The next one is at 8.40. It is 8.20 now, and she is running out of the house.

Example Sentences:

1) She won't be able to catch the 8.15 bus.
2) She'll have to catch the 8.40.

Situations:

a) Bob has just broken his leg. He wanted to play football this evening.
b) Tom likes to put cream in his coffee, but they've only got tinned milk.
c) Frank wanted to leave work early today. He wanted to see a football match. The boss asked all the men to do overtime.
d) Deborah and Arthur wanted to drive to France, but the car broke down yesterday. Deborah has just booked 2 plane tickets, instead.

2. Conversation

Mr Kent, Julia's boss, is talking to Julia on the office phone.

MR KENT: Do you think you could possibly work late this evening, Miss Frost? I'm afraid there's some work we really must finish this evening. I can't possibly do it myself.

JULIA: Work late? I . . . I suppose so, if you really think it's necessary.

MR KENT: Thank you. We'll have to work about an hour's overtime. That's all. (hangs up)

JULIA: (to herself, while dialling) Oh, dear. Now I'll have to ring Jim and tell him. He won't like it.

JIM: Hello? 26721.

JULIA: Is that you, Jim? This is Julia. Look . . . I'm afraid I won't be able to meet you at 7 this evening. I'll have to come later.

JIM: What? You mean you're going to be late again?

JULIA: Now listen, Jim, please. It isn't my fault. I'll have to work late this evening and then I'll have to go home. I can't possibly go to the restaurant straight from work!

JIM: It's always something, isn't it? When will you be able to come, then?

JULIA: Don't worry. You won't have to wait long. I'll be there at 8.

JIM: At 8? But we're going to a film after dinner. Remember?

JULIA: I know . . . and it starts at 8.30. We'll just have to miss it this evening, that's all. We'll be able to see it some other time.

JIM: Oh, no we won't! Tonight's the last night!

JULIA: Oh, dear . . . I suppose I'll just have to come straight from work, that's all.

JIM: Yes, you will. Meet me at the restaurant at 7!

JULIA: All right, Jim. I'll be there.

Questions

1. What does Mr Kent ask Julia to do?
2. How exactly does he ask her to work late?
3. Where is Julia going to meet Jim?
4. What does she want to do before she meets him?
5. What are her exact words when she tells Jim this?
6. What does she say when Jim tells her about the film at 8.30?
7. Ask if they will be able to see the film tomorrow! (and answer)
8. What does Julia finally decide she'll have to do?

e   Summary

Focal points in this Unit.

1. Remember how we use *will* when asking
   someone to do something:
   'Will you post this for me?'/'Will you carry
   this for me?'
   –and how we use *I'll* when we offer to help
   someone do something:
   'I'll post it for you.'/'I'll carry that case
   for you.'

2. Remember what we say when someone offers
   to help:
   'Thank you. That's very kind of you.'
   nice
   good
   helpful

3. Remember the Future forms of *can* and *must*:
   'I will have to see him tomorrow'/'I will be
   able to work late tomorrow.'
   'I won't have to take the test.'/'I won't be
   able to come tonight.'
   The short answers to questions like 'Will you
   be able to . . .?' and 'Will you have to . . .?'
   are *Yes, I will* and *No, I won't.*

4. Remember the emphatic pronouns:
   myself, yourself, himself, herself, itself,
   ourselves, yourselves, themselves.–as in
   'Perhaps we can do it ourselves.'

f   Exercises for homework

1. Do all the exercises on pages 81, 82 and 84.

2. **Invention Exercise**

   Write 2 sentences for each of the prompts,
   one sentence with 'I'll . . .' and one with
   'Will you . . .?'

   Example:

   that case = a) I'll carry that case for you.
   b) Will you carry that case for me?

a) that letter
b) the tickets for the concert
c) a porter
d) old car
e) medicine
f) the dog
g) some tea
h) a newspaper
i) to the cinema
j) the telephone

3. **Guided Composition**

   Write two short personal notes (only 4 or 5
   lines – not long letters!):
   a) to a friend, saying that you are sorry you
      won't be able to go to the cinema with
      him or her as arranged (and give a reason).
   b) to your boss (or teacher) explaining why
      you won't be able to do a certain piece of
      work (and give a reason).
   Before you write the notes, read situations 3,
   5 and 6 (on page 81) and the Conversation
   (on page 84) again, and notice how we use
   the following phrases which you will need:

   I'm afraid . . .//I can't possibly . . .//I'll
   have to . . .//my fault//I'll just have to . . .//
   some other time//I won't be able to . . .,
   either//I suppose . . .//

4. **Transfer Exercise**

   Write true sentences about yourself, relatives
   or friends, using 'will/won't have to' and 'will/
   won't be able to'.

   Examples:

   I won't be able to play tennis tomorrow.
   My father will have to sell his car soon; it's
   already fifteen years old.

Present perfect + 'Just'
(+ preview of contrast with simple past)

1

(a) What/police/ ticket collector?

(b) train/yet?

2

(a) Who/Peter/ with?

(b) How long/ bathroom?

(c) What/Tom/ want?

3

(a) Sun shining/ started?

(b) rain/now?

4

(a) What/Arthur's secretary/ask?

(b) Where/Mr Tigers?

(c) catch him?

5

(a) Where/Julia?

(b) What/noticed?

(c) What/just said?

(d) boyfriend's question?

(e) Julia's answer?

6

(a) Which film/ Peter?

(b) Who/noticed?

(c) Where/boy friend?

(d) Peter's question?

(e) Julia's answer?

| He (etc.) HAS | (JUST) DONE | I MIGHT | Unit **15** |
| We (etc.) HAVE | | I THINK/HOPE SO/DON'T THINK SO | |

a

1

The police are asking the ticket collector about a man they think might be on the London train.
  "Have you seen this man?"
  "No, I haven't. I mean, I don't think so."
  "Has the London train left yet?"
  "No, it hasn't."

1. Why are the police asking the collector about the man in the photograph?
2. Ask and answer the questions!
   a) London train/yet
   b) ticket collector/the man
3. Is the ticket collector sure?
4. What exactly does he say?

2

Peter is staying with Tom and Susan. He has been in the bathroom for half an hour. Tom wants to get in and has just asked "Have you finished yet?"
  "Yes, I have. I'll be out in a second," is Peter's answer. He has had a shower and has just shaved.

1. Who is Peter staying with?
2. Where is he now? Ask "How long"!
3. What has Tom just asked?
4. Ask and answer questions about Peter!
   a) finished yet
   b) a bath or a shower
   c) shaved

3

It was raining when Arthur started the conference. He has just noticed that it has stopped and that the sun has come out.
  "Look! The rain's stopped. It might be fine this evening."
  "I hope so," the other man is saying.

1. What was the weather like when the conference started?
2. What two things have just happened?
3. What has Arthur just said?
4. Is he sure it is going to be fine?
5. What is the other man's answer?

4

Arthur's secretary has just stopped another secretary in the corridor.
  "Have you seen Mr Tigers?" she wants to know.
  "Yes, I have. I saw him only a moment ago. He's just gone down that corridor." She might catch him if she hurries.

1. What has Arthur's secretary just done?
2. What does she want to know?
3. Has the other secretary seen him?
4. Ask when (and answer)!
5. What has Arthur just done?

5

Julia has just come out of the cinema. She has just noticed she has not got her umbrella.
  "I've left it inside!" she has just said.
  "Are you sure you had it when we came in?" is her boyfriend's question.
  "Yes, I am. At least, I think so."

1. What have Julia and her boyfriend just done?
2. Why has Julia suddenly stopped?
3. What does she think she has done with her umbrella?
4. What is her boyfriend's question?
5. What is her answer?

6

Peter has seen the same film, too. He has just noticed Julia. Her boyfriend has gone back into the cinema. Peter is sure he has seen her before. "Excuse me," he has just said, "Haven't we met somewhere before?"
  "No, I don't think so," is Julia's answer.

1. Why is Peter in front of the cinema?
2. Why has he stopped?
3. What has he just said and why?
4. What is Julia's answer?

Unit 15
b

---

1 Pronunciation

Notice that *have* and *has* are frequently pronounced either with the [ə] vowel-sound or with no vowel-sound at all. Study the examples. Practise them in class and notice the teacher's pronunciation and intonation.

Examples:

i) We've ['v] just arrived.

ii) Have [həv] you eaten?

iii) He's ['z] just arrived.

iv) Has [həz] he arrived?

2

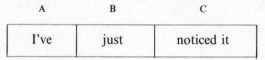

	A	B	C
	I've	just	noticed it

i) You know what sort of words can go into box A so look at the situations on page 87 to find words to go in box C.

ii) Make six sentences from the words you have found.

iii) Now make questions using the same words you used for exercise ii.

Example: Have you just noticed it?

3

	A	B	C
	Have you	finished	yet?

i) Find words to replace those in boxes A and B. You can find them in the situations on page 87.

ii) Now, ask two questions about each situation on page 87.

Example: Have the police found the man yet? (situation 1).

---

4 Use *might* for future possibilities: (See situations 3 and 4).

Make sentences from these prompts:

i) rain soon. come tomorrow. buy a new one. see the film. ask her. get one. lose it. sell them.

ii) Now think of some things you might do in the future.

---

5 Notice how we use the words THINK and HOPE to say *yes*.

Question: Will the weather be fine tomorrow?   Answer: I think *so*. I hope *so*.

But, be careful how we say *no* with these words.

Question: Will it rain tomorrow?   Answer: I *don't* think *so*. I hope *not*.

THE MAN WHO ESCAPED
Episode 15

SYNOPSIS: *Kate has come back to the flat with some clothes for Coke and other things. The Chief Inspector has told Baxter that Coke might be innocent.*

1 First Kate dyed Coke's hair grey. Then she used some theatrical make-up to give him a much older face. Finally she put a pair of dark glasses on him, thrust a white walking-stick into his hand and led him firmly to a full-length mirror. Coke was surprised at how strong her grip was. He was even more surprised when he saw himself. An old blind man 5 stared back at him.
"And now," Kate said, "You'll have to do far more than simply look like an old blind man. You'll have to walk, talk and act like one, too!" For the next hour she taught him exactly how to do that.
"You learn fast. We can go now," she finally said. 10
"What do you mean 'we'? You can't come with me. It might be dangerous," he objected. Kate was already putting her coat on. Her answer was simple. "If you want my help, you'll have to take me with you. Besides, things are just beginning to get interesting!"

2 They were walking towards a taxi-rank. There were usually several 15 taxis parked there, waiting for customers.
"We must look an odd couple, you and I," Coke remarked.
"Don't worry about that. We look so odd that nobody will guess who you are. Now just tell me where we're going!"
"To a pub in Soho called 'The Green Rider'. Masters used to go there 20 a lot," Coke answered.
"You mean you think he's one of the spies?"
"I don't know, but he didn't tell the truth at the trial. Why else should he lie?" Coke said. Just then they got to the taxi-rank. There were not any taxis there. "We'll have to take a bus. Just remember that 25 you're an old, blind man. I'll help you get on and get off!" Kate said.

3 They got to Soho half an hour later. The streets were brightly-lit. There were people, pubs, restaurants, cinemas and strip-tease clubs everywhere. There was a man in front of one of the clubs. Whenever someone passed by he said: "The best show in London. Twenty 30 beautiful girls. Step right in!" He began to say that when he saw Coke but as soon as he noticed Coke's dark glasses and white walking-stick, he closed his mouth again. They walked on until Coke suddenly gripped Kate's arm very hard. "This is the place. Take me in!" he said.
There were two doors. One was marked 'Public Bar' and the other 35 'Saloon Bar'. "Which one?" she asked.
"The Saloon Bar!" he whispered. They went into the crowded, noisy, smoke-filled room. Several people stared at them curiously when they came in.

1. **Conversation**
(for Paired Oral Practice)

Read this conversation, and use the prompts to make others like it.

Example:

MODEL: A: I've just been to the new Chinese restaurant.
B: Oh! Have you? I've just been to an Indian restaurant.

Prompts:

a) A: a new French car
   B: a German car
b) A: a book by John Wyndham
   B: a book by Nevil Shute
c) A: a new job in London
   B: a new job in Bristol
d) A: lunch in the new canteen
   B: lunch in the café round the corner
e) A: the film at the Odeon
   B: the film at the Plaza
f) A: a concert on Radio 2
   B: a play on Radio 3

2. **Conversation**

Deborah has a car of her own. There is something wrong with it. She has just driven into a garage.

MECHANIC: Good morning, Mrs Tigers. What can we do for you?

DEBORAH: I'm afraid there's something wrong with the car. I've just noticed that it's been using a lot of petrol lately; far more than usual.

MECHANIC: Oh? Well, we'd better have a look at it, then, hadn't we? Can you leave the car with us now?

DEBORAH: I suppose I'll have to. Do you think it might be something serious?

MECHANIC: I shouldn't think so. You never know, of course. It might be the engine.

DEBORAH: I certainly hope not. I want to use the car this evening. Do you think I'll be able to? I mean, will it be ready by then?

MECHANIC: It might be. It all depends on what the trouble is. Do you think you could give us a ring around 5? We'll know by then.

DEBORAH: Around 5? All right.

AT FIVE O'CLOCK THAT EVENING

SECRETARY: Good evening. Central Garage.

DEBORAH: Good evening. This is Mrs Tigers. I'm ringing about my car.

SECRETARY: Oh, good evening, Mrs Tigers. The men have just finished your car. It's ready now.

DEBORAH: Oh, good! What was the trouble?

SECRETARY: It wasn't anything very serious. There was a leak in the petrol tank. Anyway, they've taken care of it now and you can collect your car any time.

DEBORAH: Good. When do you close this evening?

SECRETARY: At 6.

DEBORAH: I see. I'll be there by then. Good bye.

SECRETARY: Good bye.

Questions

(When Deborah takes the car to the garage in the morning)
1. Correct the statements:
   a) Deborah noticed the trouble several days ago.
   b) The mechanic says the car will definitely be ready in the evening.
   c) He thinks it is something serious.
2. Answer the questions:
   a) Why does she hope it is not anything serious?
   b) What are the two things the mechanic asks her to do?

(When Deborah rings at 5)
1. Correct the statements:
   a) The men have not finished the car yet.
   b) The garage closes at 7.
2. Answer the questions:
   a) What exactly was the trouble?
   b) What have the men done about it?

e   Summary

Focal points in this Unit.

1. Remember how we use the word *just* with 'has/have done'. Notice the position of the word *just:*

    'He has *just* gone down that corridor.'
    Remember that we use *just* with 'has/have done' when we are talking about something that happened a few seconds ago.

2. Remember that we also use 'has/have done' when we are talking about something in the past, but give no indication of the time, such as the word *When,* or 'last year' or '6 months ago':

    Example:

    'Have you seen this man?'

3. Notice the form of the verb after *might:*
    'It might *be* fine this evening.'
    Remember that *might* is the same for all persons, and that we can use it in the present and in the future. In a sentence like 'They think he *might be* on the train', *might* means 'is possibly'; in a sentence like 'She *might catch* him if she hurries', 'might catch' means 'perhaps will'.

4. Remember these phrases with *think* and *hope.* Notice the different way we form the negatives:

    'I think so.'   'I hope so.'
    'I don't think so.'   'I hope not.'

f   Exercises for homework

1. Do all the exercises on pages 87, 88 and 90.

2. Change the form of these verbs and put them into the appropriate sentence.
    see; leave; come; go; meet; notice; stop; take; tell; be.

a) Haven't I . . . that girl somewhere before?
b) Have you . . . care of that noise in the engine yet?
c) He's . . . in the bathroom a long time!
d) Good! It's . . . raining. We can go out in the garden again.
e) Has he . . . you his favourite story?
f) Oh, dear! It's going to rain and I've . . . my umbrella at home.
g) 'Where's Bill?' 'Oh, he's . . . to the cinema.'
h) Have you . . . the new film of 'Hamlet'?
i) I've just . . . from a very important meeting.
j) I've just . . . that Mary has dyed her hair.

3. **Guided Composition**

Read the first half of the Conversation between Deborah and the mechanic on page 90 again, and then write a conversation between a woman and an assistant in a watchmaker's shop. There is something wrong with the woman's watch and she has just taken it in for repair. Use as many of the phrases and sentence patterns as you can, and begin like this:

WOMAN: Good morning.
ASSISTANT: Good morning, madam. What can I do for you?
WOMAN: Well, I'm afraid . . .

4. **Transfer Exercise**

Write 5 sentences about things which *have just happened.* Do not write anything which is not true.

Examples:

We have just done exercise 2.
I have just spoken to my girl/boyfriend on the phone.
My parents have just gone out for the evening.

Present perfect and past simple

1

(a) What/Julia/just?

(b) What/Julia/ask?

(c) Julia's questions?

(d) the answers?

2

(a) Who/Peter/talk to?

(b) Peter's questions?

(c) the girl's answers?

3

(a) What George Upwell?

(b) Who/talk to?

(c) ever:
cognac?
factory?
soldier?
cowboy?
prison?
teacher?

4

(a) When:
cognac?
prison? etc.

(b) George Upwell's answers?

5

(a) Deborah ever: Rome? etc.

(b) When/Rome? etc.

(c) Deborah's answers?

1

Julia has just come to work. She is late again.
She is asking one of the typists about her boss.
He often comes in late, too.

"Has the boss come yet?"

"Yes, he has. He's in his office now."

"When did he come?"

"He came very early. He noticed you weren't
here."

1. What has Julia just done?
2. Ask these questions about her boss:
   a) yet   b) early or late
   c) What/notice

2

Peter Atkins is talking to one of his girl friends.

"Have you seen that film yet?"

"Yes, I have. I saw it last week."

"What did you think of it?"

"I didn't like it very much."

1. Ask these questions about Peter's girl friend:
   a) the film yet   b) When
   c) like it

3

George Upwell is a famous writer. He has done
a lot of things in his life. He is talking to a
television interviewer now. "I've smuggled
cognac, sold used cars and worked in a factory.
I've been a soldier, a waiter and a cowboy.
I've also been in prison. I've even been a
teacher!"

1. What is George Upwell?
2. Ask these questions about him:
   a) many things   b) many places
   c) many jobs
3. Ask questions with "Has he ever . . .?"
   a) cognac   b) used cars   c) factory
   d) soldier   e) waiter   f) cowboy
   g) teacher   h) in prison

4

The interviewer is asking him when he did all
these things. "When did you smuggle cognac?
When were you in prison?" "I smuggled
cognac in 1950. I was in prison in 1951."
The interviewer is going to ask him some more
questions.

1. What are the interviewer's first two questions?
2. What are Upwell's first two answers?
3. Ask some more questions about his life with
   "When . . .?" and answer them.

5

One of Deborah's friends is asking her about all
the holidays she has had and all the places she
has been to.

"Have you ever been to Rome?"

"Yes, I have. I was there in 1967."

"Have you ever been to Mexico City, or to
Rio?"

"Yes, I've been to all those places."

"Oh? When were you in Mexico City . . .
and when were you in Rio?"

1. What is Deborah's friend asking her about?
2. Ask questions about Deborah first with
   "Has she ever . . .?" and then with
   "When . . .?" (and answer the questions)!

1 Pronunciation

i) The weak (unstressed) forms of *has* and *have* are normally used in questions starting 'Have you . . .?', 'Has she . . .?', etc.

Example: Have you ever driven a car? : [həv] you ever . . .?
Has he ever been here before? : [həz] he ever . . .?

ii) Remember: *have* and *has* at the end of a sentence are not pronounced in the weak form.

Example: Yes, I have. No, she hasn't.

iii) When was that? is usually pronounced with the weak form of *was*–[wəz].

Example: When [wəz] that?

2 Look at these verbs: (They come from the last five units.)

	1		2		1		2
see	–	saw	–	seen	come	–	came	–	come
leave	–	left	–	left	stop	–	stopped	–	stopped
go	–	went	–	gone	run	–	ran	–	run
meet	–	met	–	met	write	–	wrote	–	written

i) Read the following conversation. Observe where verb-forms like *saw* (1) and *seen* (2) are.

A: 'Have you ever seen that film?'
B: 'Yes, I have.'
A: 'When did you see it?'
B: 'I saw it last week.'

ii) You can use other time expressions to answer: 'When did you see it?'.

Example: in 1968. last year. yesterday. two weeks ago. a minute ago. a couple of days ago.

iii) Use the verbs in columns 1 and 2 and the time expressions in exercise ii to make a dialogue like the one in exercise i. Look at the situations on page 93 to make further dialogues.

iv) Now, practise using 'When was that?' in place of 'When did you see it?', and make dialogues as in exercise iii.

THE MAN WHO ESCAPED
Episode 16

SYNOPSIS: *Kate has made Coke up to look like an old blind man. They have just gone to a pub in Soho. Coke thinks he might find Masters there.*

1   Kate led Coke to a table and then went to the bar to get their drinks.
"I've been here before. I was here last week," she said when she came
back. Coke was not listening.
"Masters isn't here," he said.
"Surely you didn't expect to walk in and find him, just like that?"   5
"No, I suppose not."

Time dragged. They sat there for over an hour. More people came in,
but Masters was not among them. It was getting towards closing time
when the barman came to their table.
"May I have your empty glasses?" he asked politely.   10
Coke touched him on his sleeve. "Does a man named Eric Masters
ever come in here?" he asked. He did not notice the man standing at
the bar who stared at him in the mirror when he mentioned Masters'
name.

2   The barman thought for a second. "There's a man named Eric who   15
comes in here a lot. He's a military type. Is that who you mean?" he
asked. Coke tried to sound casual when he asked his next question.
"Has he been in here today?" The barman nodded. "Yes," he answered.
"He was in this afternoon." "I don't suppose you know where I can
find him now?" Coke asked. "I'm afraid not. All I know about him is   20
that he has an antique shop somewhere near Red Lion Square," he
answered.

"Wasn't that a bit dangerous?" Kate asked after the barman left.
"Yes, it was. But I haven't got much time. I've got to find Masters
before the police find me," he answered.   25
"I still don't understand why you can't simply find his address in the
telephone book!"
"I've already looked. I went through the phone book in your flat.
Masters might have a phone but his number isn't there."

3   The barman was shouting "Last orders, please" when Coke and Kate   30
left. Kate led him through the crowded, bright streets. Most of the pubs
were closing. It was 11.00, but the clubs and restaurants were still busy.
When they got to Shaftesbury Avenue, Kate called a taxi. Neither she
nor Coke noticed the man who was so close behind them in the crowd
that he heard Kate say "Red Lion Square, please" to the driver. They   35
did not see him get into a cab and follow them, either.

Unit 16
d

1. Invention Exercise

1) Make questions from the prompts with this model:

Example:

MODEL: Have you ever . . .?
PROMPT: spaghetti
RESPONSE: Have you ever eaten spaghetti?
       or: Have you ever cooked spaghetti?

Prompts:

a) America
b) Danish lager
c) that book
d) a jet plane
e) a Japanese film
f) the Queen
g) that girl to the cinema
h) a Rolls-Royce
i) vodka
j) any stories by Somerset Maugham

2) Now use the questions you have made to begin conversations. Use this model:

MODEL: A: Have you ever been to America?
       B: Yes I have.
       A: When were you there?
       B: I went there last year.

2. Conversation

Julia is in the watch department of a large store.

JULIA: Excuse me. Do you do watch-repairs?

SALESMAN: Yes, we do, madam.

JULIA: Oh, good. Would you look at mine? It's stopped.

SALESMAN: Certainly. Hmm . . . when did it stop?

JULIA: Only yesterday. Can you do anything about it?

SALESMAN: I think so. Just leave it with me.

JULIA: Good. When will it be ready?

SALESMAN: This time next week. Now, you'll need a receipt.

JULIA: Oh, yes. I mustn't forget that, must I?

SALESMAN: No. You won't be able to claim the watch without it.

JULIA: Good. Thank you. Good bye.

SALESMAN: Good bye. Wait a moment, madam! You've dropped something. Madam! You've dropped something! Madam!

ONE WEEK LATER

SALESGIRL: May I help you, madam?

JULIA: I hope so. It's my watch. I brought it in to be repaired but now I've lost the receipt.

SALESGIRL: Lost the receipt? Oh, dear. That *is* bad.

JULIA: Can't I just describe the watch to you?

SALESGIRL: I'm afraid not. Only the manager can help you and he's gone to lunch. He left only a minute ago.

JULIA: Oh, dear. I think it was the manager who served me.

SALESGIRL: Just a moment. When did you bring the watch in?

JULIA: This time last week, during my lunch hour.

SALESGIRL: And was your watch a small gold *Timamatic?*

JULIA: Yes, that's right. How did you know?

SALESGIRL: Because your receipt's still here. You dropped it when you left. The manager shouted but you didn't hear.

Questions

1. What does Julia say about her watch when she brings it in?
2. What is the manager's exact question when she says this?
3. According to the manager, why does Julia need a receipt?
4. What exactly does he shout when she leaves?
5. Why is the receipt still there when Julia comes back?

Recall

Without looking at the text, try to remember those parts of conversation between the salesgirl and Julia a week later.

SALESGIRL: help?

JULIA: hope. watch. to be repaired. the receipt.

SALESGIRL: bad. only the manager. just/lunch. a minute ago.

e   Summary

Focal points in this Unit.

1. In this Unit, we have practised and contrasted two tenses, the Present Perfect 'has/have done' and the Simple Past *did*.
   a) Just look again at the types of sentences we have practised with 'has/have done':
      i) 'She has *just* come to work.'
      ii) 'Has the boss come *yet*?'
      iii) 'He has done a lot of things *in his life*.'
      iv) 'Have you *ever* been to Rome?'
      (There is no mention of a specific time)
   b) And look at the types of sentence we have practised with *did*:
      i) '*When* did he come?'
      ii) 'I saw it *last week*.'
      iii) 'What did you think of it (the film)?'
      (The speaker knows *when* the other person *saw* the film; there is a definite time element)

2. Look at these two sentences:
   a) 'He's *gone* to lunch.'
   b) 'I've *been* out to lunch.'
   Sentence a) tells us that he is not here now; he is probably eating now.
   Sentence b) tells us that the person has gone to *and come back* from lunch.

3. Remember that the question 'What did you think of it?' means 'What was your opinion of it?'

f   Exercises for homework

1. Do all the exercises on pages 93 and 96.

2. Supply the correct form of the verb ('have done' or 'did') in brackets.
   a) I . . . my old car last week. (sell)
   b) . . . you . . . anything from your brother yet? (hear)
   c) We . . . John's new car. (just see)
   d) So you're back at last! Where . . . you . . .? (be)
   e) They . . . a lot of wine last night at the party. (drink)
   f) Excuse me! I think you . . . this purse a moment ago. (drop)
   g) He . . . out of the lesson a moment ago. You can speak to him now. (come)
   h) He's still in prison because he . . . cognac last year. (smuggle)
   i) . . . it . . . raining yet? (stop)
   j) Who . . . you the last time, madam? (serve)

3. **Guided Composition**

   You are a radio reporter and you have just been sent to Hyde Park where there is some trouble. Write down what you say as you commentate on the scene, paying attention to the use of 'is/doing', 'has/have done', 'has/have been doing' and 'did'.
   Begin like this:

   'I arrived here in Hyde Park about 10 minutes ago. There is a large crowd of about 200 people here. . . .'

   Finish the short report by describing how the police came, and how all the people left without violence, using these prompts:

   an hour or more//most/standing/some/sitting/grass//at the moment/very peaceful//young man/just finish/speech//start/half an hour ago//

4. **Transfer Exercise**

   Write a number of sentences about yourself using these examples:

   I've never been to China, *but I've* been to Japan. *That was* 3 years ago.
   I've never worked in a shop, *but I've* worked in a factory. *That was* last year.

Frequent gerund constructions

1

(a) When/phone?

(b) Who/person/
speak to?

(c) When/Arthur/
back?

(d) secretary/
saying?

2

(a) Why/Tom/the
dishes?

(b) Where/Susan?

(c) Tom/like/
dishes?

(d) Tom saying to/
Peter?

3

(a) When/Fred/
army?

(b) Fred/like/
soldier?

(c) Where/Fred/
now?

(d) Fred saying
to Sergeant?

4

(a) Where/Frank?

(b) What/he/give
up?

(c) Who/talk to?

(d) Frank saying
to Susan?

5

(a) Chairman shouting now?

(b) a few minutes ago?

1

The phone rang a few seconds ago. Someone wants to speak to Arthur.

"I'm awfully sorry," his secretary is saying. "Mr Tigers has gone out. He'll be back at 3. Would you mind phoning then?"

1. Ask and answer the questions!
   a) When/the phone   b) Arthur there
   c) When/back
2. The person on the phone can speak to Arthur at 3; what does Arthur's secretary say to the person?

2

Tom Atkins has to do the dishes because Susan's father is in hospital and she has gone to visit him. Tom does not like washing dishes. In fact, he hates washing them.

"I wonder if you'd mind helping me?" he is saying to Peter.

1. Ask and answer the questions!
   a) Why/Tom/the dishes
   b) like . . .?
2. What is it that he hates doing?
3. What is he saying to Peter?

3

Fred Collins joined the army a few months ago. He does not like being a soldier. In fact, he hates it. He hates carrying a heavy rifle and wearing a uniform. He also hates getting up early. All the other soldiers have already got up. "I wonder if you'd mind closing that window, Sergeant?" Fred is saying.

1. Ask and answer the questions!
   a) When/the army   b) like/a soldier
2. Ask if he hates doing these things!
   a) a heavy rifle   b) a uniform
   c) up early
3. What is he saying to the sergeant?
4. Why do you think the sergeant is angry?

4

Frank Martin is in hospital. He has had to give up smoking and drinking beer, too. The doctor says these things are very bad for him. Susan is visiting him now. "Susan, I wonder if you'd mind bringing some cigarettes next time?" he is saying to her.

1. What are the two things Frank cannot do in hospital?
2. What has he had to do? Ask why!
3. What is he saying to Susan now?
4. Do you think she will?

5

This is a political meeting. It has got out of control. The chairman is telling people to stop doing certain things. At first he tried to be polite. "Would you mind not waving that red flag?" he said a few minutes ago. Now he is shouting "Stop waving that red flag!" A group of men are shouting "freedom", two others are blowing trumpets, another group is singing and a few men are fighting.

1. What sort of meeting is this and what has happened?
2. What did the chairman say to the man with the flag a few minutes ago?
3. What is he shouting now?
4. He tried to be polite with the other people, too. What do you think he said to them?
5. What do you think he is going to shout at the other people?

---

1 Intonation

a) Notice the secretary's intonation, situation 1, page 99 'Would you mind phoning then?'
Practise saying this just as she does. Then use the same intonation pattern in the following
sentences:

  i) Would you mind sitting there?
  ii) Would you mind coming in?
  iii) Would you mind going out?

  iv) Would you mind drinking tea?
  v) Would you mind asking him?

b) Notice the very polite form 'I wonder if you'd mind . . . -ing?' Practise the intonation of this
form as Tom uses it in situation 2, page 99. Notice the way *wonder* is stressed in order to make
the question very polite. Use the three examples in situations 2, 3 and 4 on page 99 to practise
this.

---

2 Make questions (with and without *not*)

Would you Would they Would she Would he	mind	(not)	waiting for me coming back later having a new one seeing him tomorrow	?

---

3 With someone else, practise asking and answering the questions using the following very frequent
short answer forms:

  i) Yes, I (etc.) would.
  ii) No, I (etc.) wouldn't.
  iii) Not at all.
  iv) Of course not.

  v) Of course he (etc.) would ('nt).
  vi) I expect so.
  vii) I don't think so.

---

4 Using the table below, ask questions. Use the answers given in **3** to work with someone else.

I wonder	if	you'd they'd she'd he'd	mind	helping me opening the door asking her coming in	?

---

5 Using these verbs – *stop, give up, hate, like,* make sentences about these things: cigarettes, dancing,
T.V., cinema, sports cars, gardens, flowers, wine, work, swimming, football, cricket.

THE MAN WHO ESCAPED
Episode 17

SYNOPSIS: *Coke has just found out that Masters owns an antique shop somewhere near Red Lion Square. He and Kate have gone there in a taxi. They do not know they are being followed.*

1 "Would you mind driving round the Square once?" Kate asked the driver. Red Lion Square was deserted. There were a number of dark side streets around it.
"It's obviously not on the Square itself," Coke said.
They got out of the taxi, paid the driver and started exploring.   5

There were antique shops on several of the side streets but they all either had names like "Connoisseur's Corner" which told them nothing about who owned the shop, or other names like "Richards", and "Harvey Keen". Masters' name was not among them.

2 Half an hour later they were still looking. Kate kept glancing over   10
her shoulder. She had the uncomfortable feeling that someone was following them but she could not see anybody.
"I don't like wandering round the dark streets at this hour," she said.
"Someone's bound to notice us!" she went on. "I don't like doing it, either, but what else can we do? We can't stop looking now. It might   15
be our last chance," Coke answered.

Suddenly something in the window of a shop across the road caught his eye. The street was very dark but the thing gleamed. It reflected the light of a passing car. They crossed the street. The thing was an old military sabre and it was in a window marked "Antique Weapons and   20
Military Antiques." There were old pistols, helmets and other swords in the window. Coke became excited. "This must be it!" he said. Kate lit a match so that they could see a bit better. There was no name on the window but there was a phone number on the door. Coke copied it down.   25

3 It was around midnight when the phone rang in Eric Masters' flat. The voice on the other end was hard and cold.
"This is Hugo," it said. "Why didn't you come to the Green Rider?"
"I'm sorry, Hugo. I . . . I don't enjoy going there any more. Not since Coke escaped. I . . . I thought it might be dangerous." Masters was   30
nervous. He became even more so when he heard what Hugo had to say.
"There was an old blind man in the pub. He had a young woman with him. He asked about you and then went to your shop." Masters blinked in surprise. His voice cracked slightly. "But I don't know anybody like that. What did they want?"   35
"How do I know, you fool? Just watch out for them, that's all!" Hugo said furiously and hung up. Masters slept very badly that night.

Unit 17

d

FURTHER PRACTICE

1. Invention Exercise

MODEL: Would you please STOP . . . ing . . .?

1) Make questions with *stop* using the prompts:
Example:

PROMPT: that terrible noise
RESPONSE: Would you please stop making that terrible noise?

Prompts:

a) those letters
b) that guitar
c) the radio
d) those cheap cigarettes
e) the phone so much
f) your dictionary
g) so many sweets
h) that book
i) that song

2) Now use the same prompts for examples with the verb MIND:

Example:

that terrible noise – Would you mind not making that terrible noise?
those letters – Would you mind typing those letters now, please?

2. Conversation

Julia and Jim are in a pub. They are standing at the bar. In English pubs, you always have to go to the bar to get your drink. Nobody will ask you what you want if you sit down at a table first. Jim has just paid for their drinks.

BARMAN: And here's your change, sir.

JIM: Thank you.

JULIA: Can we sit down somewhere, Jim? I don't like standing here.

JIM: All right. Look! There's a table over there. Come on.

JULIA: (sitting down) This is much more comfortable. I think women look terrible standing at the bar.

JIM: Really? I don't think so. Anyway, cheers!

JULIA: Cheers!

JIM: Would you like a cigarette?

JULIA: No thanks. I've decided to give up smoking.

JIM: Really? Why?

JULIA: Well . . . it's just that I think if you don't enjoy doing something any more you should stop doing it.

JIM: I see. You mean you don't enjoy smoking any more?

JULIA: That's right. You should give it up, too. It's bad for your health.

JIM: Stop talking like my mother. That's what she keeps saying.

JULIA: But it's true. It's a nasty habit. I can't think why I ever started. Anyway, it's obviously got you in its grip!

JIM: What do you mean? What are you talking about?

JULIA: I mean you couldn't give it up!

JIM: Who? Me? Couldn't give up smoking? Nonsense! Of course I could! I know I could!

JULIA: How do you know?

JIM: Because I've already proved it. Smoking's the easiest thing in the world to give up. I've done it hundreds of times!

Questions

1. Why does Julia want to sit down somewhere?
2. What does Jim say just before he takes his first sip from his drink?
3. What has she decided to give up?
4. Ask and answer why she has decided to give up smoking?
5. What does Jim say when Julia tells him he should give up smoking?
6. Correct these statements:
   a) Jim thinks giving up smoking is very hard.
   b) Jim has never given up smoking.

Recall

Without looking at the text, see if you can remember some of the things Jim and Julia said.

JULIA: think/women/terrible/bar.
JIM: a cigarette?
JULIA: No/decided.
JIM: You mean/don't enjoy/any more?
JULIA: right. you should/too. health.
JIM: Stop/mother. keeps.
JULIA: Nasty habit. you/grip.
JIM: nonsense. easiest thing. hundreds of times.

e Summary

Focal points in this Unit.

1. In this Unit, we have practised a small number of the verbs which are followed by the '-ing' form (or the Gerund) of a verb:

   mind; hate; like; give up; stop; enjoy; keep (on).

   Remember these sentences:

   a) Would you *mind helping* me? Would you *mind not waving* that red flag?
   b) Tom *hates washing* dishes.
   c) Fred *does not like being* a soldier.
   d) Frank has had to *give up smoking*.
   e) *Stop waving* that red flag!
   f) You mean *you don't enjoy smoking* any more? ⎫
   g) That's what my mother *keeps saying*. ⎭ from the Conversation, page 102,

2. Remember how we sometimes begin a sentence with 'I wonder . . .' when we want someone to do something, and we want to be very polite:

   'I wonder if you'd mind closing the window'

f Exercises for homework

1. Do all the exercises on pages 99, 100 and 102.

2. Complete these sentences:

   a) I've just given up . . .
   b) Why don't you stop . . .
   c) Do you like . . .
   d) Do you really enjoy . . .
   e) We don't mind . . .
   f) I hate . . .
   g) You really ought to give up . . .
   h) Shall I stop . . .
   i) Will you please stop . . .
   j) I wonder if you'd mind . . .

3. Give advice to these people. Use 'You'd better give up/stop . . .'

   a) A friend who spends all his money.
   b) A man who is putting on weight.
   c) A light sleeper who always drinks coffee before he goes to bed.
   d) A young girl who always drives very fast.
   e) A student who has an exam next month, but who goes out every evening.

4. **Guided Composition**

   a) Read situation 3 on page 99 again, and then, using the prompts, write about this person:

      John Roberts/bank/3 years//not like/ bank clerk//In fact . . .//money/smart suit//also/to work early//other clerks/ already there//'I wonder . . ./earlier?' the manager has just asked him.

   b) Read situation 5 on page 99 again, and then write a radio commentator's report of the meeting. Use the patterns and vocabulary in the situation. (Remember, you did one like this in Unit 16).

5. **Transfer Exercise**

   a) Write 5 true sentences about things you *like, enjoy* or *hate* doing.
   b) Write 5 true sentences using *stop* or *give up*.

   Examples:

      I gave up riding a motor-bike a year ago.
      I stopped studying Physics when I left school.

Unit **18**

a

Future simple with 'If' or 'When' and present simple clause

1

(a) What/Fred/ about to do?

(b) What/another?

(c) Why/Fred/not jump?

(d) What/if?

2

(a) What/ millionaire/ ask?

(b) she/make up/ mind?

(c) asking him?

3

(a) What/student/ ask?

(b) What/ conductor/say?

4

(a) What/Julia?

(b) When/other typists?

(c) What/manager/ worried?

(d) manager/angry/ if?

5

(a) Which team/win?

(b) What/if/draw?

(c) How/players?

1

Fred is about to jump across the stream.
Another soldier has just fallen into it. Fred
does not want to jump. He is afraid he will fall
into it, too. He will get very wet if he does.
Fred will be very happy when all this is over.

1. What is Fred about to do?
2. What has just happened?
3. Why doesn't Fred want to jump?
4. Ask and answer these questions!
   a) Fred/wet/falls
   b) happy/over

2

The old millionaire has just asked the young
blonde to marry him. She can't make up her
mind. Perhaps she will, perhaps she won't.
   "Will you give me all your money if I marry
you?" she is asking him.

1. What has just happened?
2. Will the blonde marry him?
3. What can't she do?
4. What exactly is she asking him?

3

This foreign student does not know London
at all. He has just asked the bus conductor to
tell him when they get to Hyde Park. The
conductor is saying, "Don't worry! I'll tell
you when we get there!"

1. Where does the foreign student want to go?
2. What has he just asked the conductor to do?
3. What is the conductor saying?
4. What do you think was the student's exact
   question?

4

Julia is working late this evening. All the other
typists left five minutes ago. The manager is
leaving, too. He is worried about the lights.
   "Don't worry! I'll turn them off when I
leave," Julia is saying.
He will be very angry if she forgets.

1. What is Julia doing?
2. Why aren't the other typists there?
3. What is the manager worried about?
4. What is Julia saying to him?
5. Ask and answer the question!
   a) manager angry/forgets?

5

There are only a few minutes left in this match
between Liverpool and Manchester. Manchester
are winning by three goals to two, but they
have not won yet. Liverpool might score again,
and if they do, the result will be a draw. If that
happens, the Manchester fans will be very
unhappy. The players are very tired. They will
be very happy when the match is over.

1. What is going on here? Which team is
   winning?
2. What may Liverpool do? Ask and answer:
   Liverpool win/score?
3. Ask some more questions and answer them!
   a) Liverpool score/a draw
   b) Manchester fans happy/Liverpool
   c) players happy/over

FORMATION AND MANIPULATION

---

1 Pronunciation

These are short forms: *I'll, he'll, she'll, we'll, they'll* and *it'll*. Notice that short forms are not used in questions: 'Will you give me all your money, if I marry you?' (Situation 2, page 105.)

2

I'll	turn them off	if when	I leave.

Notice that we use 'if' when we cannot be sure that the thing is going to happen:
He will (he'll) get wet *if* he does. (Situation 1, page 105.)
Notice that we use 'when' when we know that the thing is going to happen:
I'll tell you *when* we get there. (Situation 3, page 105.)

---

3 Transformations

Make sentences using *when* or *if*.
Examples: Perhaps it will (it'll) rain. He'll get wet.
   HE'LL GET WET IF IT RAINS.
   She knows he's arriving. She'll meet him.
   SHE'LL MEET HIM WHEN HE ARRIVES.

i) I know I'll see John. I'll tell him then.
ii) Perhaps I'll see John. I'll tell him then.
iii) Perhaps I'll marry that man. He'll give me £50,000.
iv) We know it'll get dark. We'll turn on the lights then.
v) I'm going to bed. I'll turn off the lights then.

4

Will you	give me all your money	if when	I marry you?

5

Yes, I will (no short form)
No, I won't

---

6 Make sentences, ask questions and answer them. Work with someone else. Ask and answer as many questions as you can.

I'll do it	if when	you	come ask me pay me £50

Will you	come be here wait stop	when if	I	ask you tell you phone you see you	?

THE MAN WHO ESCAPED

Episode 18

SYNOPSIS: *Hugo has told Masters an old blind man and a girl have been looking for him. Coke and Kate have found what they think is Masters' antique weapon shop.*

1   Coke did not sleep very well that night, either. He lay awake thinking. He was on Kate's sofa in the sitting-room. Slowly, however, he formed a plan in his mind. He fell asleep around three in the morning.

When he woke up, Kate was already in the kitchen making breakfast. "What are we going to do now?" she asked while they were eating.   5
Coke did not answer immediately. He stared into his coffee. He knew he had to make one thing clear to her. "Have you thought what'll happen to you if the police find me here?" he suddenly asked. Kate looked at him coolly. "We've been over this before, haven't we? Now answer my question," she answered.   10
"But they'll send you to prison if they learn you've helped me!"
"I'll worry about that if and when it happens."

2   "All right. I'll tell you. But I warn you, if anything goes wrong, you might get hurt, badly hurt!" he told her.
"Go on. I'm listening."   15
"We're going to try to get Masters to come here. That is, if the owner of that shop is Masters."
"Get him to come here? How?"
Coke began to explain the plan he had in mind.

Eric Masters was cleaning an antique pistol when the phone rang in   20
his shop. He heard a young woman's voice at the other end. "I believe you buy and sell antique weapons," she said.
"Yes, that's right. I'm particularly interested in old firearms."
"My father is, too. He has a number of 17th-century pistols and he wants to sell some of them. Would you be interested?"   25
"Certainly. If you bring them to my shop, I'll look at them and give you a price."
"Well, unfortunately my father's blind. It's very difficult for him to get about. Would you mind coming to our place?" the woman answered.

3   Masters managed to answer calmly.   30
"Well . . . er . . . my assistant is out to lunch. I'll come over when he comes back. Is that all right?" He noted down the address she gave him and hung up. His hands were trembling slightly. "These must be the people Hugo told me about," he thought. He reached into a drawer and took out a pistol. This one was not an antique. It was a small, black,   35
nasty-looking automatic.

1. Practice Situations

Make one sentence for each of the situations.
Use: 'I'll (do) . . . IF . . .' or: 'I'll (do) . . .
WHEN . . .'

Examples:

SITUATION: a) Sally is going to arrive at 10.30.
You'll be at the bus-station to
meet her.

RESPONSE: I'll meet her when she arrives.

SITUATION: b) It might rain tomorrow.
I'll take my umbrella then.

RESPONSE: I'll take my umbrella if it rains
tomorrow.

Situations:

a) Cigars are definitely going to go up in price.
You'll stop smoking then.

b) It might snow tomorrow. You'll stay at home
then.

c) The weather might get better. You'll go out
then.

d) You know a telegram is coming. You'll
tell me the news then.

e) You are working in the garden. It might
rain soon. You'll go indoors then.

f) Sir Arthur is definitely going to phone soon.
You'll speak to him then.

2. Conversation

Peter Atkins has just got on a bus. He wants to
go to a place where he has never been before.
In most English buses, you usually pay after
you have got on and sat down.

CONDUCTOR: Fares, please. Any more fares?

PETER: Hatfield Road, please.

CONDUCTOR: Hatfield Road? Four, please.

PETER: Oh, will you tell me when we get there,
please?

CONDUCTOR: You'll see it yourself if you keep
an eye open. It's only a few stops from here.
Here's your ticket.

OLD MAN: I'll tell you when we get there, young
man. It's my stop, too.

PETER: Thank you. That's very kind of you.

OLD MAN: Don't mention it. These young bus
conductors won't give you any help even if

you ask politely. It was different when I was
young.

PETER: Yes, I'm sure it was.

OLD MAN: And these young bus drivers are even
worse. This one will kill us if he doesn't
slow down!

PETER: Yes. I suppose he *is* driving a bit fast.

OLD MAN: Look. Do you see those traffic lights
ahead? We'll turn left when we get to them.
Hatfield Road's the next stop after that. Why
do you want to get off there?

PETER: I want to go to the new Technical
College.

OLD MAN: Oh? You'll never find it if you go
down there alone. I'll show you where it is if
you carry one of my bags for me.

PETER: Well . . . er . . . thanks all the same but
I'm sure I can manage. I mean, I don't
want to put you to any trouble.

OLD MAN: Oh, it's no trouble at all. I have to go
past there anyway. We're almost there now.
Now, I'll carry this small bag if you take that
big one. Hurry up or we'll miss the stop!

PETER: It's . . . it's very heavy.

OLD MAN: In fact, it'll be easier to show you the
College if you take both bags. I'll have both
hands free then.

PETER: I . . . I . . .

OLD MAN: Oh, don't thank me. I'm always ready
to help a stranger!

Questions

1. Where does Peter want to get off? Ask why!
2. What exactly does he say to the conductor?
3. What does the conductor tell Peter?
4. What does the old man say he will do?
5. What does Peter have to do?

Practice

Explain in class exactly what these phrases
mean. Then practise their pronunciation and
intonation using the teacher or tape recorder as
a model:

a) Don't mention it.
b) Thanks all the same.
c) I'm sure I can manage.
d) I don't want to put you to any trouble.

e   Summary

Focal points in this Unit.

1. Remember the important difference between *if* and *when* in sentences like these:
   a) 'Fred will get very wet *if* he falls into the water.'
   b) 'Fred will be very happy *when* all this is over.'
   In a), Fred might fall into the water. It is not certain, so we use *if*.
   In b), Fred knows that all this will finish soon, so we use *when*.

2. Notice particularly the form of the verb in the *if* or *when* part of the sentence:
   a) 'Will you give me all your money *if I marry* you?'
   b) 'I'll tell you *when we get* there.'

3. The word *if* can come at the beginning or the middle of a sentence. Notice that we use a comma in the sentence only if the *if* comes at the beginning.

   The Manchester fans will be very unhappy if Liverpool scores again.
   If Liverpool scores again, the Manchester fans will be very unhappy.

f   Exercises for homework

1. Put the verbs in brackets ( ) in the correct form. They are all future ideas.
   a) I (be) there when she (arrive).
   b) If you (ask) him politely, he (help) you.
   c) What (happen) to me if I (tell) them?
   d) If prices (go up) again, I (stop) smoking.
   e) Will you tell me when breakfast (be) ready?
   f) If you (catch) the 10.30 tomorrow, you'll be in Bristol at 12.00.

2. Put the phrases in this list into the right column (1 or 3):

   you come, I'll be there, you arrive on time, the weather is fine, we'll meet you, I'll be very pleased.

1	2	3
	if	

   Now write at least 5 sentences from the table you have completed.

3. **Guided Composition**

   You have just moved to a new house in a different town. Write a short letter (about 70 words) to a friend in the old town inviting him (or her) to your new home for a weekend in the near future. Suggest the bus or train he (or she) might catch, and where and what time you can meet. Begin your letter like this:

   'Dear . . .,
   You know we have just moved into our new house here in . . ., so I am writing to ask . . .'

   Use these phrases and patterns in your letter, too:

   I'll meet you . . . if you come on . . ./If you stay . . ., we'll go out . . ./We won't be able to . . ./You'll never find it if . . ./ It'll be easier to . . . if . . ./You'll be able to tell me . . . when we . . ./

4. **Transfer Exercise**

   Write a number of true sentences about yourself using 'I'll . . . if/when . . .'

   Examples:

   I'll go to the beach this afternoon if the weather is fine.
   I'll buy a new pair of shoes when I get my wages at the end of the week.

1

(a) What/girl's father?

(b) What/he/at the moment?

(c) What/if she doesn't?

2

(a) Why/girl's mother angry?

(b) What/she/to father?

3

(a) What/Tom want?

(b) What/Susan want?

(c) Why?

(d) What/say?

4

(a) Where/Fred?

(b) ill?

(c) Sergeant/ believe?

(d) What/Sergeant/ do?

5

(a) When/Peter/ Canada?

(b) Who else/on plane?

(c) What/at Customs?

6

(a) Where/girl?

(b) early?

(c) What/if teacher?

(d) What/before?

WANT			MAKE		
ASK	}	someone *to* do	LET	}	someone do
TELL					

1

The girl's father wants her to stop playing. He wants her to wash her hands and face and eat her lunch. At the moment he is asking her to do these things. If she does not do them, he will tell her to do them.

1. What does the girl's father want her to stop doing?
2. What else does he want her to do?
3. What is he doing at the moment?
4. What will he do if she does not do these things?

2

The little girl's father told her to stop playing a few seconds ago, but she hasn't The girl's mother has just looked in. She is angry. "Make her stop! Don't let her play any longer!" she is saying to the girl's father.

1. What hasn't the little girl done?
2. What did her father do a few seconds ago?
3. What does the girl's mother think the father should do?
4. What does she think he shouldn't do?

3

Tom wants to read a book but Susan won't let him. She wants him to read something in the paper. It is an advertisement for a better job.

"Put that book down a second and look at this! Why don't you apply for this job?" she is saying.

1. What won't Susan let Tom do?
2. What are the three things she wants him to do? (book. paper. the job)
3. What does she want him to stop doing?

4

Fred is on a march. He is not really ill but he wants the Sergeant to think he is.

"Let me sit here a bit, Sergeant. I feel terrible!" he is saying.

Unfortunately the Sergeant does not believe him. He is going to make Fred get up again. He is going to make him march with the others.

1. What does Fred want the Sergeant to think?
2. Ask why (and answer)!
3. What does Fred want the Sergeant to do?
4. What exactly is Fred saying?
5. Ask three questions about the Sergeant beginning "Is he going to . . .?"
   a) Fred/up again   b) sit there
   c) march (use 'let' or 'make' with the questions)

5

Two months ago, when Peter flew back from Canada, there was a very pretty girl on the same plane. When Peter went through Customs they made him open his case. They made him take everything out. They did not make the girl do these things. They let her go through without any trouble.

1. When did this happen?
2. What did they make Peter do?
3. Ask two questions about the girl beginning "Why didn't they make her . . .?"
4. What did they let the girl do?
5. Ask why they didn't let Peter do this!

6

Here is the girl again. She is at a language institute in London. She got up late this morning. Her class has already started. She does not want the teacher to notice her. If he does, he might not let her stay. He made her go out again when she came late before.

1. Why is the girl in London?
2. Ask two questions about her!
   a) early or late this morning
   b) already started
3. What doesn't she want the teacher to do? Ask why (and answer)!
4. What happened once before?

Unit 19
b

FORMATION AND MANIPULATION

---

1 Pronunciation

Don't forget to use the weak (unstressed) form of *to* [tə].
Example: The girl's father wants her [tə] stop playing.

---

2 Notice the type of word we put in each box:

A	B	C	D	
The boss	wants	me	to work	late this evening

i) Think of some words of your own to put in box A ('The boss'). Change 'wants' to 'want' where necessary. Make full sentences.

ii) What other words can we put in box C ('me')? Make at least 6 sentences by changing 'me' to other words, like 'him', 'us', etc.

iii) Now think of other words to go in box D ('to work'). Make sure they are infinitives. Don't use 'late this evening'. Again, make full sentences. (*Example:* He wants me to finish these letters).

iv) Finally, change box B. Make sentences with 'wanted', 'ask/asked' and 'tell/told'.

3

A	B	C	D	
People today	let	their children	do	all sorts of things that children couldn't do before.

i) What are some of these things? Make sentences of your own beginning: 'They let them . . .'

ii) Are there things you think parents shouldn't let their children do? What are they?

---

4 Make sentences from this table.

A	B	C		D
He She They	wanted asked 'll tell	me him them John	to	come in go away give up smoking help her
He She	made let	John them		do it wait

---

5 i) Now think of things that your parents wanted you to do when you were young. Make sentences beginning:
'They wanted me to . . .'

ii) Now ask someone else questions beginning 'Did your parents want you to . . .?

iii) What were some of the things your parents *made you do?*
Make at least five sentences.

THE MAN WHO ESCAPED
Episode 19

SYNOPSIS: *Kate has asked Masters to come to her flat. She has told him that her father has some antique pistols he wants to sell. Masters is suspicious and has decided to take a small automatic pistol with him.*

1 Masters rang Hugo just before he left his shop.
"You told me about an old blind man and a woman . . . well, they've just phoned. They want me to go to their place and look at some antique pistols," he said nervously.
"Well, what do you want me to do about it?" Hugo asked sarcastically.   5
"You have a pistol, haven't you? There isn't much an old blind man and a woman can do to you?" he added.
Masters could not understand why Hugo was so casual about it. He got into his white Jaguar and drove off.
"Perhaps the old man really does want me to look at his pistols," he   10
thought. He patted the pistol in his pocket. It made him feel safer.

2 He felt even safer when Kate opened the door. She was slim, almost delicate-looking. "Good afternoon," he said. "I'm Eric Masters. You rang my shop earlier." She smiled. "I hope I haven't put you to any trouble. However, I'm sure you'll decide we haven't made you come   15
all this way for nothing," she said pleasantly, and led him into the sitting-room. Masters glanced suspiciously at the old, blind man sitting on the sofa. At first he seemed harmless enough, but there was some-thing familiar about the man's face that made Masters look more carefully at him.   20

"I'll go and get the pistols," Kate said. Masters stayed where he was, where he could see everything and where nobody could come in behind him. The old, blind man did not move. He simply sat there, his hands folded on his white walking-stick, his eyes behind the dark glasses staring blindly in front of him.   25
"Are you a collector, too?" Masters asked. The old man simply nodded. The woman came out of the bedroom with a large black case. "They're all in here," she said. "If you come over here, to the table, we can look at them. My father doesn't really want anyone else to have them, but I'm afraid we have no choice. It's a question of money."   30

3 Masters kept his eyes fastened on the old man's face as he walked towards the table. He was halfway there when the old man raised his face slightly. The sudden movement made Masters stop. The more he looked at that face, the more suspicious he became. Suddenly it dawned on him. He stared at both of them. They were both waiting   35
expectantly for him to come nearer. It was the old man's nose and lips that made Masters think of Coke. He reached for his pistol.

1. Invention Exercise

1. MODEL: I can't go out tonight.
   Someone wants me to do something.

Example:

PROMPT: my wife/some letters

RESPONSE: I can't go out tonight. My wife
wants me to write some letters.

Prompts:

a) The boss/some extra work
b) My teacher/a composition
c) My father/his car
d) My mother/the kitchen
e) My teacher/a lecture on the radio
f) My parents/to a concert
g) My friend/a special programme on T.V.
h) My younger brother/his homework

2. MODEL: Would you please $\begin{Bmatrix} ask \\ tell \end{Bmatrix}$ someone to do
   something?

Example:

PROMPT: Mary/the kitchen door

RESPONSE: Would you please tell Mary to
close the kitchen door?

   or: Would you please ask Mary to
open the kitchen door?

Prompts:

a) Julia/the window
b) that student/the lights on
c) Julia/me before she goes
d) Mr Smith/my office
e) them/more quietly
f) that boy/here
g) him/my bicycle
h) her/the 1967 reports

2. Conversation

It's a fine spring day. Tom is sitting in his
garden at home, marking some books.

SUSAN: Tom? Do you think you could come
into the kitchen for a second? There's
something I'd like you to look at.

TOM: What? Just let me finish these books and
I'll be right there.

SUSAN: Would you mind coming right away,
please? It's the washing machine. It's making
a funny noise. I want you to listen to it. I'm
worried.

TOM: Oh, no! Not again. (In kitchen now. Tom
has to shout above a loud whirring and
pumping noise) It's the pump, that's what it is.

SUSAN: I can't hear you. Let me turn the
machine off!

TOM: The pump isn't working properly. What
do you want me to do about it?

SUSAN: What do I want you to do about it?
Repair it, of course. You don't think I made
you leave your work for nothing, do you?

TOM: But I'm not a mechanic. Why don't you
ring the shop where we bought the thing?
Ask them to repair it!

SUSAN: Are you sure that's what you want me
to do?

TOM: Of course I'm sure! Why do you ask?

SUSAN: Because the last time they came you got
very angry.

TOM: Did I?

SUSAN: Yes. It was a small question of money.
Don't you remember? The men were only
here for half an hour but they still charged
£2 for an hour's work. You didn't like that
at all.

TOM: Oh? Hmm . . . yes, I remember now.

Questions

1. Why is Susan worried about the washing
   machine?
2. What exactly does she want Tom to do about
   it? Ask why!
3. What does he want her to do?
4. What happened the last time something
   went wrong with the machine?
5. When Susan first asks him to come in, Tom
   wants to finish the books he is marking;
   what does he say to Susan?

e   Summary

Focal points in this Unit.

1. Remember the form of the verbs which follow the verbs *want, ask* and *tell*:

'He *wants* her
to wash her
hands.'
'Why don't you
ask them *to*
repair it?'
'He *told* her *to*
stop playing.'
} want
  ask   + Infinitive with *to*
  tell

2. Remember the form of the verbs which follow *make* and *let*:

'They *made* him
open his case.'
'They *let* her *go*
through without
any trouble.'
} make   Infinitive
  let   + without *to*

3. There is an important difference in meaning between *make* and *let* as we have used them in this Unit.

'Make someone do' means 'force or cause someone to do.'
'Let someone do' means 'allow someone to do.'

4. Remember also the form of the personal pronouns we use in patterns 1 and 2 above: me, you, him, her, it, us, you, them.

f   Exercises for homework

1. Do all the exercises on pages 111, 112 and 114.

2. Choose the correct word to put in the blanks:

a) He wanted . . . to tell him the time. (my/mine/me)

b) I asked . . . to clean the car yesterday. (he/him/his)

c) Don't lɛt . . . take the books away. (they/them/their)

d) Don't ask . . . to make a cup of tea. (her/hers/she)

e) She made . . . do more work. (we/us/our)

3. Complete these sentences, using the patterns we have practised in the Unit:

a) She won't let . . .

b) Why don't you ask . . .

c) I hope he doesn't make . . .

d) If you've got the time, I'd like . . .

e) Do you really want . . .

4. **Guided Composition**

Read the second part of the Episode (lines 12–30) again carefully, and then tell about Masters' visit as Coke might have written it down later. Begin like this:

'When Masters arrived, I let Kate open the door. From the sitting-room, I heard Masters say 'Good afternoon' . . .'

5. **Transfer Exercise**

Write a number of true sentences about yourself using this model:

'I didn't want to do it myself, so I
    asked someone else to do it.
    told someone else to do it.
    made someone else do it.

Examples:

'I didn't want to do the shopping myself, so I made my sister do it.'
'I didn't want to see him myself, so I asked my friend to see him.'

Future in the past

1

(a) Why/man surprised?

(b) What/man saying?

(sure/one baby)

(never/twins!)

2

(a) When/Sheriff/saloon?

(b) Who/at the bar?

(c) Why/Jones/shoot?

(d) What/man really?

3

(a) When/millionaire/'a little present'?

(b) What/he/just?

(c) Why/she/surprised?

4

(a) Where/Peter/tell/girl friend/take?

(b) Peter/know/crowded?

(c) What/girl think?

(d) she/stay?

1

This man's wife has just had twins. Two months ago the doctor said she was going to have only one baby. The man is very surprised. "I was sure you were going to have only one baby. I never dreamt you were going to have twins!" he is saying.

1. What has just happened?
2. Why is the man so surprised?
3. Ask if the doctor knew!
4. What is the man saying?
5. Now correct the false statements like this:
   Prompt: The woman has just had a baby.
   Response: No, she has just had twins.
   a) The doctor told them she was going to have twins.
   b) The man knew she was going to have twins.

2

This is a scene from a cowboy film. Sheriff Wyatt Jones came into the Crazy Cactus Saloon a few seconds ago. A stranger was standing at the bar when Jones came in. He put his hand in his pocket and Jones shot him dead.
"I thought he was going to take out a revolver. I thought he was going to shoot me. That's why I shot him first!" Jones is saying. In fact, the man was only going to look at his watch.

1. What was the stranger doing when Jones came in?
2. What did the stranger do?
3. What did Jones do? Ask why!
4. What was the stranger really going to do?
5. Correct the statements as before!
   a) Jones knew the man.
   b) He shot him because he did not like him.
   c) He knew he was going to take out his watch.

3

A few weeks before Christmas the old millionaire told his young girl friend that he was going to give her "a little present". It is Christmas morning now. He has just given her the present. In fact, he has not given her "a little present" at all. He has just given her a large diamond ring. The girl is very surprised.
"I never realised you were going to give me a diamond ring. I thought you were going to give me a watch, or something like that!" she is saying.

1. What did he tell her a few weeks ago?
2. What day is it now and what has he just done?
3. Why is the girl so surprised?
4. Correct the statements in full sentences!
   a) The girl thought he was going to give her a car.
   b) The girl realised two weeks ago he was going to give her the ring.

4

A few hours ago Peter told one of his girl friends he was going to take her to a "quiet, elegant restaurant". They have just come in.
"I had no idea it was going to be so crowded," Peter is saying. The girl thought it was going to be an elegant place. She does not find it very elegant, at all. She wants to go somewhere else.

1. What did Peter tell the girl earlier?
2. What is he saying now?
3. What did the girl think before she came?
4. Correct the statements as before!
   a) The girl finds the place elegant.
   b) Peter knew it was going to be like this.
   c) The girl wants to stay.

---

1 Stress

Remember to use the weak (unstressed) forms of was [wəz] and were [wə] when speaking.

---

2 Notice the construction

	A	B	C
I didn't know	you	were	going to do that
	he		
	she		
	they		

What changes must we make in box B when we use words like *he, she*, etc., instead of *you*?

A	B	C
I never dreamt	you were	going to do that

  i) What other phrases can you think of to go in box A? Make complete sentences.

 ii) Make more sentences by replacing 'you were' in box B.

iii) Think of some things you didn't know were going to happen. Make sentences beginning
    'I had no idea/I didn't know/etc.' Then think of at least six other things to go in box C.

---

3 Notice the construction

A	B	C	D	E
The doctor said	she	was going to	have	only one baby

  i) Think of other words to replace 'the doctor'.

 ii) Think of other words to replace those in boxes B, D and E.

---

4 Read this. Notice the question and answer that come from it. Then, with someone else, do the same
with the other sentences.

> Julia went out at 8 without an umbrella. It began to rain at 9.
>
> Question: DID SHE KNOW IT WAS GOING TO RAIN?
>
> Answer: NO, I DON'T THINK SO, BECAUSE SHE DIDN'T TAKE HER UMBRELLA

  i) Julia ran to the bus stop but the bus came late.

 ii) Susan put on her light summer clothes. It got very cold later.

iii) Peter's girl friend put on her best clothes. He took her to a very cheap restaurant.

iv) The stranger did not even look at Sheriff Jones. Jones shot him dead.

THE MAN WHO ESCAPED
Episode 20

SYNOPSIS: *Masters has come to Kate's flat. He has just looked at Coke carefully and realised who he is. He has pulled out an automatic pistol.*

1 When Masters pulled out the automatic, Kate was standing between him and Coke. She could see that he was almost hysterical and was probably going to shoot.
"It's you! Coke!" he burst out and came nearer. Kate was standing in his way now and he put out a hand to push her away.   5
Coke could hardly believe his eyes. One moment Masters was pointing a pistol at him and the next he was lying on the floor, gasping for breath. Kate had thrown him over her shoulder. "I once played a policewoman in a film and I had to learn some judo," she said rather casually and looked down at Masters. Coke did not simply stare in   10
surprise, he gaped at her. Then he picked up the automatic that Masters had dropped and gaped again.

2 Masters groaned. He, too, could hardly believe what had happened. It all seemed incredible. He shook his head. He decided that it was probably all a nightmare, a horrible dream. He was sure that he was   15
going to wake up at any moment, safe in his own bed. He blinked his eyes several times, hoping that Kate and Coke were somehow going to disappear. He blinked again, but when he opened his eyes, they were still there.
"And now that you're here, perhaps you wouldn't mind answering   20
some questions," Coke said. Masters groaned again.
"Questions? What questions?" he mumbled. He was still in a daze.
"I want you to tell me everything that happened that evening you sent me to Epping Forest," Coke said in a low voice. Masters now realised that it was not a dream. For a moment he thought he was going to   25
be sick.

3 "I don't know what you're talking about," Masters answered.
"I think you do," Coke said.
"You can't make me tell you anything!" Masters waited to see what Coke was going to do next. He could not take his eyes off the automatic   30
in Coke's hands.
"I'll give you five seconds to begin answering my questions. Then I'll shoot," was all Coke said.
"You couldn't shoot me like that, in cold blood!"
"Couldn't I?" Coke answered, and pulled back the safety-catch. The   35
pistol was now ready to fire. Then he began counting.

1. Invention Exercise

Make sentences with:

'I thought   he/she/it was going to . . .'
'I had no idea   we/you/they were going to . . .'

Example:

PROMPT: café/so crowded
RESPONSE: I had no idea the café was going to
          be so crowded.

Example:

PROMPT: work early today
RESPONSE: I thought you were going to leave
          work early today.
      or: I thought they were going to get to
          work early today.

Prompts:

a) fine yesterday
b) programme/so uninteresting
c) tests/so difficult
d) the bill himself
e) in bed yesterday
f) her a present
g) concert/so good
h) a party tomorrow night
i) film/so bad
j) a holiday in Scotland this year

2. Conversation

In the conversation in Unit 13, Tom Atkins
described an accident he saw. A small white
Ford shot out in front of a blue car. In this
conversation we hear the two lawyers
questioning the driver of the blue car.

1ST LAWYER: Please tell the court exactly what
    happened.
DRIVER: Certainly. I was driving home along
    Harbour Road. I was just going to slow
    down when I saw a small white Ford in a side
    road. I was sure he was going to wait there
    until I drove past. I had no idea he was
    going to shoot out in front of me.
1ST LAWYER: In other words, the driver of the
    white Ford shot out without any warning, is
    that right?

DRIVER: Exactly. It was completely unexpected.
1ST LAWYER: And you had no idea this was
    going to happen?
DRIVER: No! None whatsoever!
1ST LAWYER: Thank you.
2ND LAWYER: Hmm . . . you say you were
    going to slow down when the accident
    happened, is that right?
DRIVER: Yes, it is. I was going to slow down.
2ND LAWYER: I see. I suppose you were going
    very fast at the time.
DRIVER: No, not at all! I was doing 30, that's all.
2ND LAWYER: Well, why were you going to
    slow down, then? That suggests to me, and
    I'm sure to the court as well, that you were
    going too fast in the first place.
DRIVER: No! The reason I was going to slow
    down was very simple. I was going to turn
    into the next side road.
2ND LAWYER: Really? Why?
DRIVER: Because I live there, that's why!

Questions

1. What did the driver of the blue car think the
   other driver was going to do?
2. What did the other driver do? Ask if the
   driver of the blue car knew this!
3. What makes the 2nd lawyer think he was
   going very fast?
4. Ask and answer why he was going to slow
   down!

Recall

Without looking at the text, see if you can
remember these parts of the conversation.

1ST LAWYER: any idea/happen?
DRIVER: whatsoever
2ND LAWYER: say/slow down/right?
DRIVER: Yes. down.
2ND LAWYER: very fast?
DRIVER: 30
2ND LAWYER: slow down then?
DRIVER: into the next side road. live.

e   Summary

Focal points in this Unit.

1. These are the main patterns we have learned in this Unit:

   a) I thought
   b) I had no idea
   c) I was sure   + (that)
   d) I never dreamt
   e) I never realised

   he was going to do that.
   they were going to come.

   Note that in everyday conversation, we nearly always leave out the word *that*.

2. Remember too how we use 'was/were going to do' after the verbs *say* and *tell*:

   a) The doctor said she was going to have only one baby.
   b) He told his young girl friend that he was going to give her a little present.

3. Remember the other pattern with 'going to' used by the driver in the Conversation on page 120:

   'I was just going to slow down when I saw a small white Ford . . .'

   Notice the position of the word *just*.

f   Exercises for homework

1. Do all the exercises on pages 117, 118 and 120.

2. Complete these sentences using 'was/were going to . . .'

   a) We didn't really know . . .
   b) The doctor didn't think . . .
   c) The driver never dreamt . . .
   d) Peter never realised . . .
   e) Tom was sure . . .
   f) We all thought . . .
   g) The girl had no idea . . .

3. Do you remember the pattern 'He . . . *so* (*well/fast/badly* etc.) that . . .'? We practised it in Unit 7. Look at these 2 sentences. They combine 'so . . . that . . .' and 'thought, etc. . . . was going to . . .'

   He *drove so fast that I thought he was going to have* an accident.
   She *played so beautifully that I was sure she was going to win* a prize.

   Now write more sentences like this using the prompts:

   a) dangerously/job
   b) slowly/late
   c) badly/walk out
   d) carelessly/the football match
   e) fast/early

4. **Guided Composition**

   Write a short story about a day that turned out badly. Begin with this sentence:

   'When I woke up, the sun was shining and I thought it was going to be a glorious day.'

   Then use these phrases for the beginnings of some of the sentences:

   'It was the first day . . .'/'As soon as . . .'/ 'When I went into the garage . . .'/'The tyre . . .'/'I never realised . . .'/'Two hours later . . .'/'She was still waiting . . .'/'Just then it began . . .'/'It was still raining . . .'/ 'The weather was so . . .'/

5. **Transfer Exercise**

   Look at the patterns in point 1 of the *Focal points in this Unit.* Use each of them to write 2 true sentences about yourself, the weather, the lesson etc.

Past perfect

1

(a) Why/police-man/man/station?

(b) Who/corner?

(c) When/arrest?

2

(a) How long ago/accident/happen?

(b) What/Peter/see?

(c) Why/police-man/man/station?

3

(a) Who/Julia/bank?

(b) Why/night-safe?

(c) What/man?

(d) Julia's answer?

4

(a) Who/ask/questions?

(b) How long ago?

(c) What/Julia/when/man?

(d) ever before then?

5

(a) Who/Arthur's office?

(b) done to his desk?

letters?

money?

lamp?

(c) Why/run away?

6

(a) Who/ask/questions?

(b) Arthur/see thieves?

(c) What/Arthur/see?

(d) What sort/mess/they?

1

One car has run into another. A policeman is taking one of the drivers to the police station because, just after the accident, the man got out and hit the other driver. Peter has just come round the corner. The policeman arrested the man a few seconds ago.

1. What has one car done?
2. Ask what the policeman is doing!
3. Ask why!
4. What has Peter just done?
5. What did the policeman do a few seconds ago?

2

Peter is talking about what he saw a few hours ago. "I saw there had been an accident. One car had run into another. When I got there, a policeman was taking one driver to the station. The man had hit the other driver. That's why the policeman had arrested him."

1. What does Peter say that shows he did not see the accident itself?
2. What had one car done?
3. What was the policeman doing? Why?
4. What had the policeman done?

3

The office manager has sent Julia to the bank with a lot of money, but it has closed. That is why she has put it in the night-safe. A man has suddenly appeared. "I want your money!" he has just shouted.

"But I've put it in the night-safe!" Julia is saying. She is very frightened.

1. What has the office manager done?
2. What has Julia done with the money? Why?
3. What has the man just shouted?
4. Why can't Julia give him the money?

4

A policeman is asking Julia questions.
"When did all this happen?"
"Half an hour ago. I'd just put the money in the night-safe when I saw him."
"Had you ever seen the man before then?"
"No, I hadn't. He was a total stranger."

1. What is happening now?
2. Why didn't the man get the money?
3. Why didn't Julia take the money into the bank itself?
4. Correct the statements!
   a) She was going to put the money into the safe when she saw the man.
   b) She knew the man.

5

Thieves have broken into Arthur's office. They have emptied his desk, thrown all his letters on the floor and have taken most of the money from the safe. They have also smashed the lamp on his desk. They are running away because they have just heard Arthur in the office outside.

1. What have they done to his desk?
2. What else have they done?
3. What are they doing now? Why?
4. Correct the statements!
   a) They have taken all the money.
   b) They have left his letters in the desk.

6

A policeman is asking Arthur questions.
"Did you see the thieves?"
"No, they'd already run away when I came in."
"What did you see when you came in?"
"Nothing, except what they'd done. They'd made a terrible mess."

1. Why didn't Arthur see the thieves?
2. Make as many sentences as you can beginning "Arthur saw they had . . ."!
3. Ask questions beginning:
   "Had they . . . when he got there?"
   Answer "Yes, they had"/"No, they hadn't."

Unit 21
b

FORMATION AND MANIPULATION

1 Pronunciation
Remember that the word *had* has a short form *'d* [d] and a weak (unstressed) form [(h)əd].

2 Study this example:

A	B	C	D	E
She had ('d)	already just	left	when he	phoned

i) Think of some words to replace 'she' in box A. (Remember that you can use words like 'Peter' and 'the bus'.)

ii) Now, think of some words to replace 'left' in box C.

iii) Now, think of some words to replace 'phoned' in box E.

iv) Using the words you have thought of write or say ten sentences using *already* or *just*.

3 Study this table:

Julia hadn't	got up washed the dishes eaten finished her work got dressed	when Jim got there

i) Use this table for this conversation. Talk with another person.

   A: 'Why did Jim have to wait for Julia?'   B: 'Because she hadn't . . .'

ii) Use the table again to ask questions like this. Talk with someone else and tell him to take B's part.

   A: 'Had Julia . . . when Jim got there?'   B: 'No, she hadn't. That's why he had to wait.'

4 Look at this conversation
   A: 'What had happened when she got there?'   B: 'They'd already left.'

Make other conversations like this with the person sitting next to you using the following prompts:

i) A: got there   B: left   iv) A: went in   B: started

ii) A: arrived   B: telephoned   v) A: rain started   B: game stopped

iii) A: saw it   B: finished   vi) A: man came   B: she gone

Now, do the same thing again using the word *just* instead of *already*.

THE MAN WHO ESCAPED
Episode 21

SYNOPSIS: *Kate has thrown Masters over her shoulder. Coke has grabbed his pistol and has told Masters he will kill him if he does not answer his questions. Coke is going to count up to five before he shoots.*

1 "But I know nothing!" Masters protested. Coke had already raised the pistol and simply said, "One!" Masters said nothing.
"Two!" Coke brought the pistol nearer.
"You can't frighten me!" Masters shouted.
"Three!" Masters saw Coke had already taken aim. 5
"How can I tell you something I don't know?" Masters demanded.
"Four!" Masters watched Coke's finger beginning to press the trigger.
"All right, all right, I'll tell you anything you want, but for God's sake, put that pistol down!" Masters gasped.

2 Coke's mind went back to the time, five years earlier, when both he 10
and Masters had been officers in the same Army Intelligence unit.
Masters had been Coke's superior. Several important military secrets
had disappeared and they were both trying to find out who had taken
them.

One evening, Coke had gone, on Masters' orders, to a lonely place in 15
Epping Forest. Masters had told him he would meet a possible informer
there. While he was waiting, three men had grabbed him from behind.
They had poured whisky all over him and down his throat and then
hit him over the head.

3 When he came to, he was back in his car, but it had crashed into a 20
tree. The police had already arrived. It appeared that Coke had got
drunk and lost control of his car. The police had found several files
marked 'Top Secret' in his car. Coke swore he had never seen them
before. The police also found Coke had apparently deposited more
than £2,000 in his bank account a few weeks before. Coke had known 25
nothing of the money. The bank said the cheques had arrived by post,
drawn on a Swiss bank, with Coke's countersignature. Nobody
believed Coke's story. It appeared he had sold secrets for money and
was going to do so again the night he had crashed. Masters denied he
had ever told Coke to go to Epping Forest. This is what Coke wanted 30
to ask questions about now.

FURTHER PRACTICE

1. For Comprehension

Read this newspaper report and then answer the questions:

LIVERPOOL UNITED VS. REAL VALENCIA
by our Football Correspondent, Hugh MacTully.

This was a wonderful match. The two teams had been playing for only 3 minutes when Gomez scored the first goal. Jimenez had almost scored a minute before.

Liverpool came back with a fine attack. Unfortunately Tarleston, their centre forward, left the field in the 35th minute. He had hurt his ankle badly earlier, but had been playing despite the injury.

Bobby Good scored for Liverpool in the 40th minute. He had taken a pass from Biles, had run 40 yards and had beaten at least 3 Valencia defenders when Torez almost brought him down with a hard tackle. Good got past him somehow, shot over the head of the goal-keeper and scored.

Final Score: Liverpool United 1   Real Valencia 1

a) How long had they been playing when Gomez scored?
b) Did Jimenez score a goal in this match?
c) Did Tarleston leave the field the moment he hurt his ankle?
d) Cover the text and write down what Good had done when he scored the equalising goal for Liverpool. (Prompts: a pass from Biles/ 40 yards/3 Valencia defenders)

2. Conversation

Arthur is at dinner with an old friend, George Tetley. George has just told Arthur a joke.

ARTHUR: (laughing loudly) That was very good. I'd never heard that one before.
GEORGE: Hadn't you? Well, here's another one like it. This one's about a travelling salesman named Phil, who was quite a whisky-drinker. Phil had gone to a strange town one day and had spent the evening in a pub. He'd drunk quite a lot and had just come out of the pub when he saw another man in the middle of the road. The other man had been in the pub, too, and had drunk even more than Phil had. He'd obviously seen something strange in the sky because he was pointing upwards. 'Excuse me,' the man asked Phil, 'is that the sun or the moon?' Phil looked at it for a second and then said, 'I'm afraid I can't help you. I'm a stranger here myself'.
ARTHUR: (laughing again) Very good. Now let me tell you one. A doctor was examining a lady who was no longer very young. She'd fallen down and had hurt her knee. The doctor wanted to be sure that that was all she'd hurt. 'Tell me,' he asked her casually, 'how old are you?'. 'Twenty-five' was the answer. The doctor wrote 'Loss of Memory' down on his notes.

Questions

1. Where had Phil spent the evening and what had he done there?
2. When did he notice the man and why?
3. What did the other man ask and what was Phil's answer?
4. Why was the doctor examining the lady?
5. What did he ask her and what did he do afterwards? Ask why!

Recall

Tell someone else both jokes without looking at the text.
Use these prompt words to help you.
Phil/strange town and/evening/pub. quite a lot/ just out when/man/road. something strange/sky. upwards. 'Excuse me'

doctor/lady/very young. fallen down/knee. doctor/sure that was all. 'How old . . .?' 'Twenty-five'. memory.

e   Summary

Focal points in this Unit.

1. In this Unit we have studied and practised the Past Perfect Tense 'had done' in sentences like – "When I got there, I saw there *had been* an accident.'
and 'They *had run* away when I came in.'
When we use 'had done' in English, we are concerned with what someone *had already done* or what *had already happened before* 'I got there' or 'I came in' etc.
We often make this more obvious by using a phrase like 'By then' or 'By the time . . .'
   Example:
   'By the time I got there, the thieves *had already escaped.'*

2. Remember the negative form –
   'He *hadn't drunk* very much.'
   and the question form –
   'Had you ever seen the man before then?'
   and the short answers –
   'Yes, I had'/'No, I hadn't', etc.

f   Exercises for homework

1. Do all the exercises on pages 123, 124 and 126.

2. Supply the correct 'had done' form of the verb in brackets:

   a) When I went back to the shop, they (sell) the book I wanted.
   b) She (visit) England only twice before she came this year.
   c) As soon as they (go), I went straight to bed.
   d) When we got to the station, we found that the 8 o'clock train (already leave).
   e) When the police got to the bank, the thief (already escape).
   f) I spoke to the woman because I thought I (meet) her somewhere before.
   g) Deborah woke up with a terrible headache because she and Arthur (hold) a party the night before.

3. Look at these two sentences:
   I had never been to America before I went there last year.
   She had never seen the Eiffel Tower before she visited Paris last month.
   Now write 5 sentences like this yourself.
   Use these verbs in the place of *been* and *seen* in the sentences above: eat, stay, drink, fly, visit.

4. **Guided Composition**

   a) Read situations 5 and 6 on page 123 again, and then write a short newspaper article (about 60 words) about the theft.

      Here is the headline:

      THIEVES BROKE INTO DIRECTOR'S OFFICE

      And begin your article:

      'At about 7.20 yesterday morning, thieves broke into the office of Arthur Tigers, director of the British Car Company. When Mr Tigers arrived at about 7.30, he found . . .'

   b) Read situations 1 and 2 on page 123 again, and then write the conversation in court one or two days later between a lawyer and Peter. The policeman had taken Peter's name and address as a witness, and Peter had to go to the court case.
      (Remember you read two Conversations like this before, one on page 78 and the other on page 120.)
      Begin like this:

      LAWYER: Now Mr Atkins, would you please tell the court what you saw when you arrived on the scene of the accident?

5. **Transfer Exercise**

   Write true sentences about things that happened to you or another member of your family or a friend yesterday. Include a 'had done' idea at the same time. Here are two examples: When I got home yesterday evening, the rest of the family had already had dinner.
   I had just gone out in the garden to sunbathe yesterday afternoon when it started to rain.

Conditional sentences

1

(a) What/in tree?
(b) Why/not run?
(c) What/they/if?

2

(a) What/ attendant/say?
(b) Tom's question?
(c) more expensive?

3

(a) What/Peter/ say?
(b) Why/Tom/use it?

4

(a) What/ 2 men?
(b) Why/difficult?
(c) What/both men/say?
(the job?)
(these axes?)

5

(a) What/not understand?
(b) Why/not/job?

6

(a) Who/live/ house?
(b) home/better/if: grass? gate? flowers?

1

These people do not know there is a snake in the tree. If they knew, they would probably start screaming and the man would drop his sandwich. If the man had a gun, he could shoot the snake.

1. Why don't the people get up and run now?
2. What would they all do if they knew?
3. Ask and answer the same type of question about
   a) the man   b) the woman
4. Why can't the man shoot the snake?
5. Now make a sentence: if/a gun/shoot.

2

"If I were you, I'd use Super Petrol. Your car would go faster if you did," the petrol attendant said a moment ago.
   "Would it really?" was Tom's question.
   "Yes, it would! Definitely!"
   "But wouldn't it be more expensive?"
   "No, it wouldn't!" is the answer.

1. What did the attendant say he would do if he were Tom? Ask why! (answer)
2. What was Tom's first question?
3. What was the answer and what did Tom ask then?
4. What is the attendant's answer?

3

Peter has just said "Would it be all right if I borrowed your car this evening? It'd help me a lot if I could use it." Tom would let him use it if he did not need it himself. He is saying: "Unfortunately, I need it myself this evening. I'd let you have it otherwise."

1. Ask and answer why Peter wants to borrow Tom's car!
2. What are the exact words of his question?
3. What is Tom's answer?
4. Ask and answer a question beginning "Would Tom . . . if . . .?"

4

These two men are trying to cut down a very large tree. Their electric saw is broken. Their axes are not very sharp. "The job would be easy if that saw weren't broken!" one man has just said.
   "These axes would be all right if they were a bit sharper!" the other is saying.

1. What are these men doing?
2. Why is it so difficult?
3. Ask and answer the questions!
   a) easy/saw
   b) easy/axes sharper

5

"I can't understand why I can't find a job!" this man is saying. He would probably find one if he got a haircut, shaved off his beard, bought a new suit, put on a clean shirt and polished his shoes.

1. What is the man saying?
2. What do you think he should do?
3. Ask and answer questions beginning "Would he find a job if . . .?"

6

Two very old, poor people live here. The house would look much better if they painted it, cut the grass, mended the gate and planted a few flowers. They would probably do this if they weren't so old and had a bit more money.

1. What sort of people live here?
2. Ask questions beginning: "Do you think the house would . . . if . . .?"
3. Now ask and answer two questions beginning: "What would they do if . . .?" (money/old)

1 Pronunciation

i) The word *would* has a short form [d] and a weak form [wəd].
Example: If I could come, I'd [d] tell you.
If I could come, I would [wəd] tell you.
ii) The word *were* has a weak (unstressed) form [wə] which is very frequently used.
Example: If I were [wə] you, I'd do it.

2 Look at and repeat these sentences:

i) If they knew, they would start screaming.
ii) Your car would go faster if you bought some.

iii) Would it be all right if I borrowed your car?
iv) If the man had a gun, he could shoot the snake.

Questions:

i) What do you notice about sentences that begin with *If*?
ii) Now, what about sentences that don't begin with *If*?

iii) Does it make any difference if the sentence is a question?
iv) So, what can you say about 'IF' and the comma?

3

A	B	C	D	E	F	G
If	the man	had a gun	,	he	could shoot	the snake

i) Look at the situations on page 129 and find words to replace those in boxes B, C, E, F and G.
ii) Now, make at least ten sentences from the new words you have found in exercise i.
iii) Now, practise starting sentences with boxes E, F and G and finishing with A, B and C.

4

a)

What could	he	do	if	he	had a gun?

b)

He	could	shoot	the snake

Look at the answers you found for exercise 3 ii and use them to make questions and answers like those above. *Example:*

a) What would you do if it rained?   b) I would (I'd) go home.

5

A	B	C
If I were you,	I'd	use super petrol

NOTE: We use this form to give advice.
Look at the situations on page 129. Give advice to all of the people.

6

A	B	C
Would it be all right if	I	borrowed your car . . .?

i) Change the words in boxes B and C. Use words like these in box C: used the phone, got up late, had a bath, came in now, saw her, etc.
ii) Think of other phrases to put in box C. (Look at the situations on page 129; you may find some help there.)

THE MAN WHO ESCAPED
Episode 22

SYNOPSIS: *Masters has agreed to tell Coke everything.*

1 For a moment Coke wanted to pull the trigger. He had never killed
anyone in cold blood, but he found it difficult not to hate Masters.
Because of him, he had lost four years of his freedom. Because of him
everybody thought he was a spy. Somehow, Coke got a grip on himself.
Perhaps it was because he knew Masters was his only chance to prove   5
he was innocent, and he knew if he killed him, he would lose that
chance.

2 "Let's start at the beginning . . . when you sent me to Epping Forest
that night," Coke said in a flat, cold voice.
"That was Hugo's idea. I had nothing to do with it."   10
"And who is Hugo?" Coke demanded.
"He sells government secrets to any foreign country that's interested.
He made me give him information. I didn't want to!"
"Made you? How did he make you?" Coke asked.
Masters stared down at the floor for several seconds before he answered. 15
"He knew things about me. He said he would tell the police about them
if I didn't help him."
"What sort of things?" Again, Masters hesitated before answering.
"What does it matter? The sort of things that would ruin any man
if the police or anyone else found out about them."   20

3 There were only a few more things Coke wanted to know now. "Why
did you involve me in all this?"
"The police suspected someone. We wanted to make them think you
were the spy. We knew they would if they found your dead body in a
car after a crash with all sorts of secrets in it."   25
"My dead body?"
"Hugo thought the crash would kill you," Masters said.
"A pity it didn't. You'd still be safe if I were dead!"
Masters swallowed and stared at the floor.
"And why aren't you still in the army? You'd be a lot more useful to   30
Hugo if you were," Coke went on.
"It became too dangerous. Anyway, he still uses me."
"How?" Coke asked.
"We hide microfilms of secret documents in the antique weapons I
send abroad. The people we send them to pose as foreign collectors."   35
Coke had one last question. It was the most important. "Where's
Hugo now? Take me to him!"

1. Invention Exercise

Write sentences with 'If . . . (did) . . . would (do) . . .':

Example:

PROMPT: that film/it

RESPONSE: If you saw that film, you'd enjoy it.
   or: If they went to see that film, they'd enjoy it.

Prompts:

a) by bus/to work earlier
b) that house/some flowers and trees
c) my car/on time
d) a haircut/a job
e) super petrol/much better
f) less/more money
g) better meals/healthier
h) a car/you to London
i) more carefully/fewer mistakes
j) enough money/theatre this evening

2. Conversation

Arthur's secretary has told him she would like to see him about something personal. She has just come into his office.

ARTHUR: Sit down, Miss Bradley. It's something personal, you say?

MISS BRADLEY: Yes. You see, I'm going to get married next month and . . .

ARTHUR: Get married? I didn't know that. Congratulations!

MISS BRADLEY: Thank you, but I'm afraid it means I've got to give in my notice. I'd like to leave at the end of the month.

ARTHUR: Really? I'm very sorry to hear that. Do you intend to stop working altogether, then?

MISS BRADLEY: Oh, no! My fiancé and I want to save up enough for a house and we wouldn't be able to do that if I stopped working right away. And it isn't that I don't like my job here, either. I'd stay if Terry, that's my fiancé, weren't a Canadian.

ARTHUR: A Canadian? I'm sorry, I don't understand. What's that got to do with it?

MISS BRADLEY: Well, we're both going to live in Canada as soon as we get married.

ARTHUR: Oh, I see. What does your fiancé do for a living, by the way?

MISS BRADLEY: He's an engineer. He often says he'd earn far more if he were back in Canada. That's why he wants to go back.

ARTHUR: But engineers are quite well paid here in England. How much does he earn here, then, if I may ask?

MISS BRADLEY: £20 a week.

ARTHUR: Is that all? That's very poor for a qualified engineer. You ought to tell him he'd get far more if he came and worked for us.

MISS BRADLEY: Well . . . er . . . you see . . .

ARTHUR: I mean, I'm sure that if I were a young engineer and if my salary were that low, I'd want to go to Canada, too. Where does he work, by the way?

MISS BRADLEY: Er . . . as a matter of fact, he works here in your factory, Mr Tigers. He's in your motor-design department.

Questions

1. Ask and answer these questions
   a) Why/her notice?
   b) stop working altogether?
   c) fiancé come from?
   d) earn?
   e) Why/back to Canada?
2. What does Arthur say Miss Bradley ought to tell her fiancé?
3. Where does he work?

Practice and Recall

Without looking at the text, see if you can remember how these phrases were used. Then try to make other sentences of your own with the same words.

a) I'm afraid it means
b) my notice
c) It isn't that I . . .
d) for a living
e) by the way
f) as a matter of fact

e Summary

Focal points in this Unit.

1. a) In this Unit we have practised another kind of Conditional sentence with the word *if*: 'If . . . did . . ., . . . would do'. This is sometimes called the unreal Conditional, because, in a sentence like– 'The job would be easy if that saw weren't broken' –the fact is that the saw *is* broken, and the job *isn't* easy.

b) The verb in the *if* half of the sentence is in the Simple Past form of the verb: 'If they *knew*, . . .'/'If he *had* a gun, . . .'/ 'If he *bought* a new suit, . . .'

c) The form of the verb in the other half of the sentence is 'would (do)': '. . . they *would start* screaming.'/'. . . it *would go* faster.'

2. Remember that we only use a comma in the sentence if it begins with *if*: 'If they painted the house, it would look a lot better'.

3. Remember the form of the verb 'to be' in this kind of sentence: 'If I *were* you, I would stay at home.' We use *were* with all persons: 'If *I were* rich, . . .'/'If *he were* in your position, . . .'/ 'If *they were* here, . . .' etc.

f Exercises for homework

1. Do all the exercises on pages 129, 130 and 132.

2. Supply the correct form of the verb in brackets in these sentences.

a) If you (work) harder, you would earn more money.

b) She (get) a much better job if she learnt to type.

c) If I (drink) a bottle of wine, I would be ill.

d) That house (probably look) very nice if they painted it.

e) I'd drink a cup of tea if you (make) some.

3. Give advice to the following people. Use: 'If I were you, I'd . . .'

Example:

A student who doesn't work very hard. Advice: If I were you, I'd work a bit harder.

a) A woman who always goes to bed very late.

b) A friend who smokes more than 50 cigarettes a day.

c) A man who is very thin and unhealthy.

d) A friend with a bicycle that often goes wrong.

e) A man who is very unhappy in his job.

f) Someone with very bad toothache.

g) A person who is trying to open a tin with a hammer.

h) A friend who has just bought a new car, and the car has just broken down.

i) A man who wants a job in Sweden, but can't speak Swedish.

4. Guided Composition

A friend of yours has written to you recently to ask your advice about a problem. The problem is that the friend wants to brush up his (or her) English, but doesn't know whether to go to a school in England for an intensive course or to go to evening classes in his (or her) home town. Write a letter advising the friend what you would do.

5. Transfer Exercise

Write down a number of things you would do right away if you won a lot of money.

1

(a) Why/house look better?

(b) Why/window?

(c) Why/gate?

(d) Why/garden?

(e) Who?

(f) When?

2

(a) When/these 3 cowboys?

(b) know who?

(c) How/Tom? How/Dick? How/Harry?

3

(a) Who/Tom's favourite record?

(b) When?

(c) Susan/record?

(d) What/Tom say?

4

(a) What/Tom/ policeman?

(b) What/happen? (bumper. headlight.)

(c) policeman's question?

(d) Tom's answer?

5

(a) When/storm?

(b) How much damage? (trees. telephone wires. windows. a roof. a car.)

(c) When/all this?

6

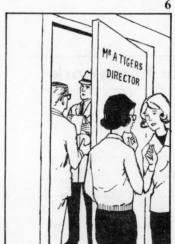

(a) When/Arthur's office?

(b) money?

(c) damage?

1

This is the same house we saw in Unit 22. It has been painted. The window has been mended. So has the gate. The garden looks better because some flowers have been planted. We do not know who did these things or even when they were done. All we can say is that they have been done.

1. What has happened to the house?
2. Ask and answer the same question for
   a) the window   b) the gate
3. Why does the garden look better?
4. There are two things we do not know; what are they?

3

Tom's favourite record has been broken. "It's been broken" he said a moment ago.

"Well, don't look at me. I didn't break it," Susan said.

"I didn't say you did. All I said was 'It's been broken,'" Tom is saying now.

1. What has happened to Tom's record?
2. What are Tom's exact words when he notices this?
3. What is Susan's answer?
4. What is Tom saying now?
5. Why do you think he does not say "It was broken"?

5

There was a terrible storm during the night. A lot of damage was done. Trees and telephone wires were blown down, windows were smashed and a roof was blown off. A car was even overturned. All this happened last night.

1. Ask and answer questions beginning "What happened to that/those . . . last night?"
2. Ask a question beginning "How much damage . . . ?"
3. Suppose you have *just* seen all these things for the first time and perhaps do not know when they happened; what would you say?

2

These three cowboys were all killed a long time ago in Cactus City. We know how they died but not who killed them. All we can say is that Tom was hanged, Dick was shot dead and Harry was stabbed, all in 1877.

1. Correct the statements!
   a) We see the houses of three cowboys.
   b) They were killed a short time ago.
2. What do we know? What do we not know?
3. Ask and answer questions beginning "How was . . . killed?" and "When was . . . killed?"

4

Tom's car has been damaged. He is telling a policeman about it.

"Look! The bumper's been bent and a head-light's been smashed!"

"Do you know when this was done, sir?"

"No. All I know is the car was all right when I parked it here three hours ago!"

1. Ask and answer three questions beginning "Does he know when . . . ?"
   a) the headlight   b) the car
   c) the bumper
2. What exactly is he saying about these three things?
3. What is the policeman's question?
4. What is the only thing Tom knows?

6

Arthur's office was broken into this morning. Two typists are talking.

"Have you heard? Mr Tiger's office has been broken into!"

"I know. It was broken into this morning."

"Was any money stolen?"

"I think so. I know some damage was done."

1. How does the first typist begin the conversation?
2. What does the other one say?
3. What exactly is the question with the words "any money"?
4. Ask and answer questions with these words:
   a) When/the office   b) How much money
   c) A lot of damage

---

1 Pronunciation

BE VERY CAREFUL WITH THE PRONUNCIATION OF THE SHORT FORM OF 'HAS' [z].

 i) After words ending like CAT, CAP, BOOK, WIFE, PATH (where the last sounds are unvoiced) 's is pronounced [s].
   Example: The cat's [kæts] been found.

 ii) After words ending like HEAD, THING, WAVE, TREE, BOY (where the last sounds are voiced, vowels or diphthongs) 's is pronounced [z].
   Example: The boy's [boiz] been seen.

 iii) After words ending like HOUSe, GAZe, FISh, CHURch, JUDge the short form *cannot* be used. Instead the full or weak forms must be used.
   Example: The house has [hæz] or [həz] or [əz] been painted.

 iv) Don't forget to use the weak (unstressed) forms of: was—[wəz] and were—[wə].

2

A	B	C
The window	has ('s) been	mended

 i) Look at the situations on page 135 and find words to replace those in boxes A and C. (Of course, you'll have to change box B sometimes.)

 ii) Now say or write at least ten sentences.

 iii) Now, try to think of five *new* things to replace those in boxes A and C.

 iv) Look at this simple dialogue   A: 'What's happened?'
                                         B: 'The window's been broken.'

 v) Using the words you have found in exercises i and iii, make these short dialogues with the person sitting next to you.
   Example: 'What's happened?'
            'My car's been stolen.'

3

A	B	C
Some damage	was	done

 i) Make at least five sentences of your own by putting new words in boxes A and C. (Change 'was' to 'were' when necessary.)

 ii) Now make those sentences into questions beginning 'When . . .?'

 iii) How many questions can you ask with 'When . . .?' about the pictures on page 134?

4

It hasn't	been done	yet

Make sentences using these words:
my watch/repair. the house/sell. window/mend. flowers/plant. radio/switch on. car/clean.

THE MAN WHO ESCAPED
Episode 23

SYNOPSIS: *Masters has told Coke that Hugo had planned what had happened to Coke in Epping Forest. He thought Coke would be killed in the crash and that the police would think he was the spy when they found the documents in his car. Coke wants Masters to take him to Hugo.*

1   Masters told Coke that Hugo owned a large garage in the North of London. Cars that had been damaged were taken there to be repaired. It was also where the secret documents Hugo sold were kept before they were micro-filmed and sent abroad.

They got into Masters' white Jaguar and drove there. Coke sat in   5
front with Masters. Kate sat behind. It was almost evening when they got to the garage. It was at the end of a street and was surrounded by shops and small houses. They parked at the end of the street. People were beginning to close their shops and go home. The garage stayed open until six. Coke sat and watched the lights go off. When the last one   10
had been turned off and the garage was completely dark, Coke turned to Masters again.
"Now tell me exactly where the documents are kept before they're sent off," he said.

2   At first Masters did not answer. He had become a little braver again.   15
Coke pressed the pistol into his stomach.
"Because of you, I've been kept in prison for four years. Because of you, my life has been ruined. I'll kill you here and now if you don't answer!"
Masters looked at the pistol and went pale.   20
"They're kept in Hugo's office, in an ordinary file in his desk," he answered. "And the microfilms?" Coke demanded. "They're kept there, too."
"Do you know if any documents have been sent off recently?"
"Some were sent last week. I know. I sent them myself," Masters   25
said. "And will there be any there now, waiting to be sent off?" Again Masters hesitated. Coke pressed the pistol even harder into his stomach. "I don't know. There might be. Hugo told me he was going to give me some soon," he said.

3   Coke gave Kate the pistol. She was still sitting behind Masters. "Keep   30
him here until I get back," he said.
"But what are you going to do?" she asked.
"Break into that garage if I can. Perhaps I can find proof that Hugo sells these things. If I do, I'll phone the police."
"But what if you don't? What if you're seen and caught before you   35
can find anything at all?" Kate asked. But Coke had already started walking towards the dark garage. In the dark winter evening, it looked very much like a prison.

1. For Comprehension

1) There has been another rail crash in Scotland. The crash occurred last night in freezing fog outside Glasgow. Four people were killed and at least ten people were injured.The railway lines have not yet been cleared and a number of trains have been delayed.

2) Heavy snow has fallen in the North of England. Many roads have been blocked and traffic has been brought to a standstill. One town, Castlepool in Yorkshire, has been completely cut off. Supplies will be dropped into the town by air this afternoon.

3) The office of Mr Arthur Tigers, the prominent industrialist, was broken into during the weekend. A small amount of money was taken and the office itself was left in what the cleaning woman described as 'a terrible mess'. The burglary was discovered by cleaners early this morning. Mr Tigers is away on holiday in South America and has not yet been located.

Questions:

1 a) Where did the rail crash occur?
 b) Were there any casualties in the crash? (killed/injured)
 c) Have the lines been cleared yet?
 d) Are the trains still running normally? (trains/delayed)

2 a) Where has heavy snow fallen?
 b) What are conditions like? (many roads/ traffic)
 c) What has happened to Castlepool?

3 a) What happened to Mr Tiger's office during the week-end?
 b) Was any money taken?
 c) How was the office left?
 d) Who was the burglary discovered by? When was the burglary discovered?

2. Conversation

Joe Burns is a famous racing-driver. He is being interviewed on a sports programme.

REPORTER: You've had a very dangerous life, haven't you, Joe? I mean, you've almost been killed several times, haven't you?

JOE: Yes. I suppose that's right.

REPORTER: When was your worst accident?

JOE: I'd say last year. It was during the British Grand Prix. I smashed into a wall. The car was completely ruined and my left leg was broken. Luckily, nobody was killed.

REPORTER: Is that the only time you've been . . . er . . . close to death?

JOE: No. Once, during the Mexican Grand Prix, two cars in front of me had a bad accident. One of them ran into the other. I swerved to avoid them and hit a fence. My car was badly damaged but luckily I wasn't even hurt.

REPORTER: You must enjoy danger. I mean, you wouldn't be a racing-driver if you didn't, would you?

JOE: I don't know about that. I had a very frightening experience quite recently. I was frightened to death! I thought I was going to be killed at any moment.

REPORTER: Really? When was that? During your last race?

JOE: No. It was on my way to this studio. I had to drive through London during the lunch hour.

Questions

1. What has almost happened to Joe several times?
2. When was his worst accident? Describe it! (wall. car. leg.)
3. What happened during the Mexican Grand Prix? (two cars. swerved. his car.)
4. What did Joe think was going to happen to him very recently?
5. When did this last experience take place?

e   Summary

Focal points in this Unit.

1. Remember that we form the Passive in English with 'to be + done'. In this Unit we have practised two tenses–'has/have been done' and 'was/were done'.

2. Remember that we use these two Passive tenses in the same way as we use the Active forms:

   a) *'has/have been done'* + *just, yet, ever, since, for* or no time.
   'The house *has been painted* (since we last saw it).'

   b) 'was/were done' + 'last night', 'yesterday', '3 weeks ago', etc.
   'Mr Tiger's office *was broken* into this morning.'

3. We usually use the Passive when we don't know or don't want to say who has done, or who did something. If we use the Passive and still mention the person, however, we use the preposition *by*, as in the third news item on page 138–'The burglary *was discovered by cleaners* early this morning.' In this sentence, the burglary is the most important piece of information.

f   Exercises for homework

1. Do all the exercises on pages 135, 136 and 138.

2. Supply the correct form of the verb in brackets (has/have been done or was/were done) in these sentences:

   a) The President (be shot) late last night.
   b) There isn't any food left. All of it (be eaten)!
   c) I can't find my car anywhere. I think it (be stolen)!
   d) Our house (be broken into) last week.

   e) Those paintings (be sold) last month for £500 each.
   f) His car (be damaged) in an accident last month.
   g) 'Have you heard? The old police station (be repainted).'
   h) That's a good book. It (be written) by George Orwell.
   i) Because of bad weather yesterday, the traffic on the motorway (be brought) to a standstill.
   j) I (be frightened) to death when I drove through Paris last month.

3. **Guided Composition**

   a) Read the first news item on page 138 again. Use that as a model and write about a bad car crash. Use these prompt words:

   car crash/Bristol//yesterday afternoon/ snow storm/near the centre//one old lady/4 other people/2 cars/completely wrecked//not cleared/traffic/held up.

   b) Now read the second news item on page 138, and write a similar article beginning:

   'Heavy rain has fallen . . .

4. **Transfer Exercise**

   Write six sentences about the news today, using the Passive.

   Examples:

   'The President of . . . arrived in . . . today, and was met by the Prime Minister.'

   '. . . was beaten by . . . in the international football match at . . . today.'

1

(a) Where/Julia and Jim?

(b) What/she/know?

(c) Julia's question?

(d) How/Jim/know/good restaurant?

2

(a) How long/restaurant?

(b) Why/Julia/angry?

(c) What/Jim/the place?

3

(a) Why/Julia/conductor?

(b) Where/money?

(c) Who/next stop?

4

(a) When/inspector?

(b) What/see?

(c) What/conductor say?

5

(a) Where/Tom?

(b) What/Susan?

(c) Susan's question: flowers?

(d) Tom's answer? (worry. forget.)

6

(a) Why/Susan/upset?

(b) What/tell Tom?

1

Julia and Jim, her boyfriend, are outside a restaurant. Julia wants to know something before they go in.

"Are you sure it's a good restaurant?"

"Oh, yes!" Jim is saying, "I've been here before. It's very good. I know the owner and I always get good service."

1. Where are Julia and Jim?
2. Correct the statements!
   a) Jim says it is a bad place.
   b) He says he has never been here before.
   c) He says he does not know anyone.
   d) He says he never gets good service.

2

Jim and Julia have been in the restaurant for an hour and they still have not been served. Julia is angry. "You said this was a good place!" she is saying. "You said you had been here before! You said you knew the owner and always got good service!"

1. Where are Julia and Jim?
2. Ask "How long . . .?" and answer.
3. Why is Julia angry?
4. What did Jim say before they came?
   a) good place   b) before
   c) the owner   d) good service

3

It is lucky Julia takes the same bus every morning and knows the conductor. This is their conversation this morning:

"I'm sorry. I've left my money at home."

"It doesn't matter. You can pay tomorrow."

Unfortunately an inspector is going to get on the bus at the next stop.

1. Why is it lucky she knows the conductor?
2. What are her exact words?
3. What are the conductor's exact words?
4. What is going to happen at the next stop?
5. Ask if the conductor knows! (and answer)

4

The inspector got on a minute ago and he wants to see everyone's ticket. Julia is explaining why she has not got one.

"I told the conductor I had left my money at home. He told me it did not matter and that I could pay tomorrow."

1. What does the inspector want to do?
2. What is Julia doing?
3. What did she tell the conductor?
4. What did he tell her?

5

Tom is going into town and Susan wants him to do something for her there.

"It's my mother's birthday tomorrow. Will you get her some flowers in town? She loves roses."

Tom is saying "Don't worry. I'll get her some! I won't forget!"

1. What does Susan want Tom to do?
2. Ask why! (and answer)
3. Ask and answer these questions!
   a) When/birthday
   b) What sort of flowers
4. What is Tom saying?

6

Tom has come back from town but he has forgotten to get the roses. Susan is very upset.

"I told you it was my mother's birthday tomorrow and that she loved roses. You said you would get her some! You said you wouldn't forget!"

1. Ask why Susan is upset! (and answer)
2. What did she tell him?
3. What did he say?
4. Correct the statements:
   a) He said he'd get them tomorrow.
   b) She said her mother's birthday was next week.

1 Notice the change:

IS/ARE/DOES

> Jim says 'This *is* a good restaurant'   Jim said it *was* a good restaurant
> Jim says 'I *know* the owner'   He said he *knew* the owner

Now make the same change yourself for these sentences that Jim says. Change them to 'Jim said . . .'

i) 'The food is good.'   v) 'The vegetables aren't fresh.'
ii) 'The waiter speaks five languages.'   vi) 'The meat tastes strange.'
iii) 'My boss often goes there.'   vii) 'The soup has a fly in it.'
iv) 'A lot of famous people eat there.'   viii) 'I don't like this place.'

2 HAS/DONE/DID

> Julia says *either* 'I've *left* my money at home'   Julia said she *had left* her money at home
>   *or* 'I *left* my money at home'

Now change these statements to sentences beginning 'Julia said . . .'

i) 'I've lost my purse.'   v) 'The manager has already come.'
ii) 'I've broken my watch.'   vi) 'The bus has just left.'
iii) 'I ate earlier.'   vii) 'The bus left 5 minutes early.'
iv) 'I knew Susan at school.'   viii) 'My alarm clock didn't go off.'

3 WILL DO/CAN DO

> Tom says 'I'*ll* get some in town'   Tom said he *would* get some in town
> Tom says 'I *can* do it later'   He said he *could* do it later

Now change these statements to sentences beginning 'Tom said . . .'

i) 'We can buy them later.'   v) 'He'll be home soon.'
ii) 'I'll remember.'   vi) 'He won't mind.'
iii) 'I won't come home without them.'   vii) 'Susan will be very angry.'
iv) 'Peter can get them.'   viii) 'I can't go home without them.'

4 SAY/TELL

Notice that when we want to mention the person we said something to, we use the word *tell*.

> I said I was coming
> I told you I was coming

Now look at pictures 2, 4 and 6 on page 140. Ask questions like 'What did . . . tell . . . earlier?'
Answer these questions with: 'He/She told her/him that . . .'

THE MAN WHO ESCAPED
Episode 24

SYNOPSIS: *Coke has gone to Hugo's garage. He has told Kate he is going to try to find proof that Hugo is a spy.*

1 Once, a long time ago, someone had told him that an Army training was useful in many ways. Coke knew now that that was true. There was a drainpipe at the back of the garage that led to the roof, and Coke managed to climb up it. He had often done such things in the army. 5

There was a window in the roof, or a sky-light, as it is called. It was closed but not locked. Coke managed to get it open and then peered down into the dark garage below. There was a lorry parked almost directly underneath. He jumped down onto it. It was completely dark inside the garage itself. 10
"Masters told me the secrets were kept in the office, but where's the office?" he wondered. Suddenly he heard a sound behind him, and realised he was not alone in the garage.

2 Before he could turn around, someone grabbed him from behind and someone else shone a powerful light into his eyes. He was blinded. 15
Then, there was an explosion of pain in his head. He realised, just before he lost consciousness, that what had happened in Epping Forest was happening to him all over again.

When he came to again, he was lying on the floor of the garage. It was at least an hour later. He heard loud voices. When he opened his 20
eyes, he saw Kate tied to a chair. Four men were standing above him. One of them was Masters, looking pale and frightened. He was listening to a short blond man. Coke knew it must be Hugo himself. Hugo was shouting.
"I told you you were a fool . . . and idiot! Do you believe me now?" 25
he demanded. Masters tried to say something but could not.
Hugo slapped him across the face.
"I asked you if you believed me now?" he shouted.

3 "But . . . but Hugo. Pl . . . please listen to me!" Masters stammered.
"I told you someone had phoned me and had asked me to look at 30
some pistols! I told you it was an old, blind man but you said there was nothing to worry about!" Masters said.
"No, I didn't. I asked you what you wanted me to do about it, you idiot!" Hugo roared. Suddenly, one of the other men interrupted.
"What did you say we were going to do with the girl and Coke?" 35
he asked.
"I said we were going to kill them! And I said we were going to do the job properly this time!" Hugo answered.

1. For Comprehension

Read this newspaper article and answer the questions.

When Mr Long, the Minister of Education, was asked about the school-leaving age again at a press conference yesterday, he said that there were still a large number of problems to be considered. One reporter asked what the Government was going to do about children who wanted to go out and earn money at the age of 16. Mr Long said that he realised a lot of young people wanted to stand on their own two feet early in life, and he thought this was very good. But he added that he felt young people needed as much education as we could give them: so the Government was seriously considering raising the school-leaving age some-time in the future.

Questions:

a) Where was Mr Long yesterday?
b) What was he asked about?
c) What did he say about 'a large number of problems'?
d) Write down the exact words which one reporter used when he asked Mr Long about the school-leaving age.
e) What did Mr Long say a lot of young people wanted to do?
f) What did he think about this?
g) What did he say about young people and education?
h) What is the Government doing now?

2. Conversation

Most of Tom's students at the Technical College are between 15 and 18. Most of them are serious students, too. A few are not. Tom is talking with one of the few now. She has just told him she can't come to school tomorrow because her grandmother is ill.

TOM: You've already missed far too many lessons this term, Miss Grey.
MISS GREY: Yes, I know I have. I'm very sorry. You see, I have these terrible headaches and . . .

TOM: Headaches? Only last week you said you had trouble with your stomach!
MISS GREY: Er . . . well . . . I have headaches *and* trouble with my stomach, you see. That's why I've been absent so often.
TOM: And you often come to college late as well. Yesterday, for instance, you . . .
MISS GREY: Yes. I'm very sorry about that. You see, my alarm clock didn't go off and . . .
TOM: Your alarm clock? But you told me yesterday that the bus had broken down!
MISS GREY: Oh, did I? Well . . . er . . . I suppose I just forgot to say that my alarm clock hadn't gone off, either.
TOM: It's a very complicated story, if you'll forgive me saying so, Miss Grey. Now, tell me again why you want tomorrow off.
MISS GREY: Well . . . er . . . you see . . . my grandfather's ill. He's in hospital and . . . and he's going to have an operation. I want to visit him.
TOM: Oh, I see. So your grandfather's ill as well.
MISS GREY: As well? I . . . I don't understand.
TOM: Neither do I, Miss Grey. When we began this conversation, you said your *grandmother* was ill. And you didn't say she was going to have an operation! You said she'd already had one! And by the way, you also said she was in an old people's home, not in a hospital!

Questions

1. Miss Grey has been absent a lot. What reason did she give for this last week?
2. What reason did she give for being late yesterday?
3. What did she say about her grandmother earlier?

Practice

Go through the conversation again. Find all the examples you can that begin with 'you said' or 'you told me'. Then say what the *exact* words were at the time Miss Grey first said these things.

e   Summary

Focal points in this Unit.

1. Remember how we use the two verbs *say* and *tell*–
   a) 'I said' is simply followed by the reported information.
   b) We add a person ('him/her/us/John', etc.) after 'I told'.
   Compare these two sentences:
   '*He said* he would be late.'
   '*He told me* he would be late.'

2. Remember that the verbs in the past of the sentence after *said* or 'told him' goes back one tense from what was said originally:

   'am/is' become 'was', and 'are' becomes 'were'; 'knows/know' become 'knew', and 'doesn't/don't know' become 'didn't know'; 'did' and 'has/have done' become 'had done'; 'can' becomes 'could', and 'will' becomes 'would'.

   Example:

   Original statement: 'I don't know.'
   Reported statement: He said he didn't know.

f   Exercises for homework

1. Do all the exercises on pages 141, 142 and 144.

2. Change these sentences into Reported Speech.
   Example:
   'I'm French,' she said.
   You write: She said she was French.
   a) 'I like tea,' she said.
   b) 'I hate it,' he told me.
   c) 'John never wears a dark suit,' she said.
   d) 'I think that is a very good idea,' he said.
   e) 'You can't get very far,' Baxter told him.
   f) 'You are a free man,' Baxter told Coke.
   g) 'I'll buy a new suit if I get the job,' the young man said.
   h) 'My car has broken down,' he told the mechanic.
   i) 'I'm going to give up smoking!' he told the doctor.
   j) 'I've just been to the optician's,' he told me when I saw him a minute ago.
   (Begin: When I saw him a minute ago, . . .)

3. Read this passage and write down exactly what they said:

   When I woke up, I asked my wife what the weather was like. She looked out of the window and said it was raining very heavily, but she thought it was going to get brighter. Later, when we were having breakfast, I listened to the weather forecast. The announcer said that the weather in the south would probably be very changeable. He added that the Meteorological Office couldn't say when the weather would become more stable. My wife said that was fine because she had decided to stay at home and do some cooking.

4. **Guided Composition**

   Read the Conversation between Tom and Miss Grey on page 144 again. Think of an excuse for being late for school, college or work. Write down how you told a friend what happened when you used the excuse to your teacher, lecturer or boss. Report what you said and what he or she said. Begin like this:

   'I was late for school (or college or work) again last . . . When I went in, . . .'

5. **Transfer Exercise**

   Report a number of things that different people have said to you in the past couple of days. For example, if a friend said to you yesterday: 'I'm going to a party tonight.'– you write:

   'My friend told me he was going to a party last night.'

Past conditional

1

(a) time now?

(b) Tom/play?

(c) Why not?

2

(a) When/Fred?

(b) other soldier's questions?

(c) Fred's answer?

3

(a) When/Peter/ from Canada?

(b) job yet?

(c) What/Tom/say?

(d) What/Peter/ think?

4

(a) Why/Jones/ dead?

(b) Jones' explanation?

5

(a) When/old lady/road?

(b) What/if/driver?

(c) What/2nd and 3rd cars?

(d) What/if/old lady/careful?

WOULD HAVE DONE IF HAD DONE

1

It is 9 o'clock. Susan has just asked "Aren't you going to watch the play?" Unfortunately Tom has a lot of work to do. "I would if I had the time" is his answer.

It is 11 o'clock. The play is over. Tom did not watch it. He would have watched it if he had had the time.

1. What is Susan's question at 9?
2. What is Tom's answer?
3. What can we say about Tom at 11?

3

Peter came back from Canada six months ago. He has not found a job yet. His brother Tom often tells him:

"You would have found a job long ago if you had looked harder!"

Peter often says: "Perhaps it would have been better if I'd stayed in Canada!"

1. Ask and answer the questions!
   a) When/from Canada?
   b) a job yet?
2. What does Tom often tell Peter?
3. What does Peter often say?

5

A few seconds ago, that old lady suddenly stepped into the road. The first car would have killed her if the driver had not stopped just in time. Unfortunately, the second car crashed into him and the third car swerved and hit the curb. The first driver has lost his temper, the second driver has damaged both cars and the third has knocked down a lamp-post. None of this would have happened if the old lady had been careful. Unfortunately the damage has been done now.

1. What happened a few seconds ago?
2. Make as many sentences as you can beginning "If the old lady had been careful . . ."
3. Ask as many questions as you can like this: "Would the first driver have stopped so suddenly if the old lady hadn't stepped into the road?" (and answer)

2

Fred joined the army 6 months ago. At that time he did not know how hard life was going to be for him. Another soldier has just asked him a question.

"Would you have joined if you had known?"
"No, I wouldn't" is Fred's answer.

1. What happened 6 months ago?
2. What was it that Fred did not know then?
3. What is the other soldier's question and what is Fred's answer?
4. Correct the statements:
   a) He would still have joined if he had known.
   b) He knew how hard life was going to be.

4

We saw this scene earlier. When Sherriff Jones came into the bar, a stranger made a sudden move. Jones shot him dead. The man only wanted to look at his watch. Jones is explaining

"I'd never have shot him if he hadn't made a sudden move. If he hadn't been a stranger, I wouldn't have been so suspicious."

1. Why was Jones so suspicious?
2. Ask and answer a question with 'if'! (suspicious/a stranger?)
3. What did the stranger do when Jones came in?
4. Ask another question with 'if' and answer! (shot him/sudden move)

Unit 25
b
FORMATION AND MANIPULATION

1 Pronunciation

i) Notice the pronunciation of *have* in the last sentence of situation 1, page 147 'He would have [(h)əv] (sometimes written *would've*) watched it if . . .'

ii) Notice the pronunciation of *had* in the last line of situation 1, page 147, where the word *had* occurs twice.

The first *had* may be pronounced in its short form ('d) or weak form [(h)əd]. BUT THE SECOND 'HAD' MUST BE STRESSED (i.e. in its full form).

Example: '. . . if he had had ['d hæd] or [əd hæd] or [həd hæd] the time.'

2

A	B	C	D	E

A	B	C	D	E
He would have	watched it	if	he'd	had the time.

i) Think of words to replace those in boxes B and E. You'll find some in the situations on page 147 and also in the other conditional situations on page 129.

ii) Look at this simple dialogue:
'Did he watch it?'
'No, he didn't, but he would have watched it if he'd had the time.'

iii) Now, using the words you have found in exercise i, make at least ten examples of the dialogue in exercise ii. You should do this orally with the person sitting next to you and also write down a few examples (two or three).

3

A	B	C	D

A	B	C	D
Would you have	joined	if you had	known?

i) By using pages 147 and 129 again, find words to replace those in boxes B and D. (You can, of course, change 'you' in A and C.)

ii) With the words you have found in exercise i, write or ask at least ten questions like the example above.

iii) Now practise asking the same ten questions starting with *if*.
Example: If you had known, would you have joined?

4

A	B	C	D

A	B	C	D
If he hadn't	been a stranger	I wouldn't have	been so suspicious.

i) Think of other words to go in boxes B and D.

ii) Change 'he' and 'I' in boxes A and D as necessary.

iii) First write or say at least ten sentences using the words you have found in exercises i and ii.

iv) Now, write the same sentences, or some new ones starting with box D.
Example: I wouldn't have been so suspicious if he hadn't been a stranger.

THE MAN WHO ESCAPED
Episode 25

SYNOPSIS: *When Coke broke in, Hugo and two other men seized him and knocked him out. That was at least an hour ago.*

1 Hugo saw that Coke had come to. Coke tried to get up but his hands were tied. His head hurt terribly. Hugo looked at him like a shark inspecting his dinner.
"We would never have become suspicious if you hadn't used Masters' white Jaguar," he said. "When we saw it parked halfway up the road, 5 we decided to wait and see what would happen. Then, after we got you, we went out and got your girl friend," he continued.

Coke knew he would never have made such a stupid mistake if he had not been so tired. He had not slept properly for days. He looked at Kate. "I'd never have got you into all this if I hadn't asked you for 10 help," he said to her. He was trapped. It seemed there was nothing he could do and nobody who could help him. Hugo took out a revolver. "You'd never have bothered us again if I'd used this four years ago," he said. He came closer to Coke and aimed the revolver carefully at his head. 15

2 Suddenly there was a terrific crash as three policemen broke down the side door of the garage. Hugo turned round and gaped. "No, Hugo. Look up here!" a voice roared from the sky-light above. Suddenly, everybody stopped. Nobody made a move. Then Baxter dropped through the sky-light, which was still open, and onto the lorry and 20 finally to the ground. Three more policemen followed him. Baxter walked over to Hugo.
"Your revolver, please," he said simply.

"I was only protecting my property," Hugo answered. "This man broke in. That girl helped him. Send him back to prison!" Baxter 25 listened and smiled. "Certainly, but only after you've given me that revolver," he replied. Hugo handed it to him silently.

3 The policemen around Baxter and at the door suddenly moved forward and seized Hugo, Masters and the three men.
"We've followed you everywhere for days; that's why we're here now," 30 Baxter told Masters. Then he turned to Hugo and said "And I've been up there for half an hour. I've heard everything you've said. Also, I think you'd have phoned us an hour ago, when Coke first broke in, if you'd only wanted to protect your property!"

Before Hugo could protest, he and the others were led away. Baxter 35 helped Coke to his feet. "What we know now already proves you were innocent," he said. Then he untied Coke's hands. Coke was a free man again.

THE END

Unit 25 d

1. Invention Exercise

Make sentences with '. . . would/wouldn't have done . . . if . . . had/hadn't done.'

Examples:

1) PROMPT: that film/time
   RESPONSE: I would have seen that film if I had had the time.
      or: We would have gone to see that film if we had found the time.
2) PROMPT: accident/asleep
   RESPONSE: He wouldn't have had an accident if he hadn't been asleep.
      or: I would have had an accident if I had fallen asleep.

Prompts:

a) that job/a haircut
b) so suspicious/a stranger
c) some flowers/enough money
d) football/leg
e) the book/the film
f) married/the right man
g) train/bus/so slow
h) money/cleverer
i) university/intelligent
j) job/carefully

2. Conversation

Peter, Tom and Susan have all gone to a very expensive restaurant. They've just finished eating.

SUSAN: I must say your roast beef looked even better than my steak. I think I would have ordered that if I'd known.

TOM: Do you mean you didn't like the steak?

SUSAN: Oh, no. Just the opposite. I enjoyed my meal very much.

PETER: Well, I'm glad you both did because I'm going to pay. Waiter!

TOM: Don't be silly, Peter! We can't let you do that.

SUSAN: No, we can't. I mean, we'd never have come to such an expensive place if you'd told us that earlier.

PETER: No, let me pay. I insist.

WAITER: Yes, sir. Did you call?

PETER: Yes, the bill please.

WAITER: Er . . . do you want the bill separate or all together?

PETER: All together, of course.

WAITER: Very well, sir. I'll be right back.

PETER: What a strange question. It's my long hair. He'd never have asked me that otherwise.

TOM: What do you mean?

PETER: Oh, it's just that all these snobbish waiters think people like me never have any money.

SUSAN: He's coming back now.

PETER: Oh, good Lord!

TOM: What's wrong?

PETER: I . . . I'm terribly sorry. I've just noticed . . . I haven't got any money. I must have left it at home. I . . . er . . . I'd never have offered to pay if I'd known. Do you think you could lend me a few pounds, Tom?

Questions

1. What would Susan have done if she had known about the roast beef?
2. What does Susan say when Peter tells them he is going to pay?
3. What does the waiter ask when Peter asks for the bill?
4. What is Peter's comment?
5. What does Peter notice just before the waiter comes back?
6. What does he ask Tom to do?

e   Summary

Focal points in this Unit.

1. In this Unit we have practised another kind of Conditional sentence with the word *if:*
'If . . . had done, . . . would have done.'
This is sometimes called the Past Conditional because when we use it, we are always talking about the past. Like the other Conditional sentence we practised in Unit 22, however, this is also *unreal*. In a sentence like 'I'd never have shot him if he hadn't made a sudden move', the fact is that the stranger actually made a sudden move, and the sheriff shot him!

2. Remember that the verb in the *if* half of the sentence is in the Past Perfect tense:
'If I *had stayed* at home, . . .'

3. Remember that the verb in the other half of the sentence is 'would have done':
'If I had stayed at home, I *would have watched* that programme on television.'

4. Remember that the shortened form of both *would* and *had* is *'d*. Look at this sentence:
'*I'd* never have done that if *I'd* known.'
(I would)   (I had)

f Exercises for homework

1. Do all the exercises on pages 147, 148 and 150.

2. Complete these sentences:
   a) If I had known, . . .
   b) We wouldn't have gone there . . .
   c) If we hadn't been in such a hurry, . . .
   d) I wouldn't have asked them . . .
   e) If the prices hadn't gone up so much, . . .

3. Make comments to the following people. Use 'I wouldn't have . . . if I had been you.'
   Example:
   A friend who failed an exam because he wasted time.
   Comment: *I wouldn't have wasted so much time if I had been you.*

a) A person who paid £500 for a car that was only really worth £250.
b) A friend who went on a 3-week holiday, but who spent all his (or her) money in the first week.
c) A man who has a bad headache this morning because he drank too much at a party last night.
d) A friend who went for an interview for a job and wore an old sweater and jeans and not a smart suit. (The interview was for an office job.)
e) A friend who was arrested by the police because he was involved in a violent political demonstration.

4. **Guided Composition**
   Look at these two sentences:
   'Coke went to Epping Forest. If he hadn't gone to Epping Forest, the three men wouldn't have attacked him.'
   Now write about other incidents from 'The Man Who Escaped' and say what the consequences would or wouldn't have been if . . . Here are some reminders:
   a) the old lady's cottage
   b) the motor-bike incident
   c) Kate's flat
   d) 'The Green Rider'

5. **Transfer Exercise**
   a) Do you remember sentences like 'I had no idea it was going to be so crowded'? We practised a lot of sentences like this in Unit 20. Write some true sentences using 'would/wouldn't have done . . . if . . . had done' + 'was/were going to'.
   Examples:
   I wouldn't have gone to the football match if I had known it was going to be so boring./We wouldn't have booked a table at that restaurant last night if we had realised how bad the service was going to be.
   b) Write a number of true sentences about yourself, friends or relatives, like this:
   'I watched a film on television last night, and it was terrible! I wouldn't have watched it if I had known.'

Irregular verbs

INFINITIVE	PAST TENSE	PAST PARTICIPLE	INFINITIVE	PAST TENSE	PAST PARTICIPLE
be	was	been	lend	lent	lent
beat	beat	beaten	let	let	let
become	became	become	lie	lay	lain
begin	began	begun	light	lit	lit
bend	bent	bent	lose	lost	lost
bite	bit	bitten	make	made	made
blow	blew	blown	mean	meant	meant
break	broke	broken	meet	met	met
bring	brought	brought	put	put	put
build	built	built	read	read	read
burn	burnt	burnt	ride	rode	ridden
buy	bought	bought	ring	rang	rung
catch	caught	caught	rise	rose	risen
choose	chose	chosen	run	ran	run
come	came	come	say	said	said
cost	cost	cost	see	saw	seen
cut	cut	cut	sell	sold	sold
dig	dug	dug	send	sent	sent
do	did	done	set	set	set
draw	drew	drawn	shake	shook	shaken
dream	dreamt	dreamt	shine	shone	shone
drink	drank	drunk	shoot	shot	shot
drive	drove	driven	shut	shut	shut
eat	ate	eaten	sing	sang	sung
fall	fell	fallen	sink	sank	sunk
feed	fed	fed	sit	sat	sat
feel	felt	felt	sleep	slept	slept
fight	fought	fought	slide	slid	slid
find	found	found	smell	smelt	smelt
fly	flew	flown	speak	spoke	spoken
forget	forgot	forgotten	spend	spent	spent
freeze	froze	frozen	stand	stood	stood
get	got	got	steal	stole	stolen
give	gave	given	stick	stuck	stuck
go	went	gone	strike	struck	struck
hang	hung	hung	swear	swore	sworn
have	had	had	swim	swam	swum
hear	heard	heard	take	took	taken
hide	hid	hidden	teach	taught	taught
hit	hit	hit	tear	tore	torn
hold	held	held	tell	told	told
hurt	hurt	hurt	think	thought	thought
keep	kept	kept	throw	threw	thrown
know	knew	known	understand	understood	understood
lay	laid	laid	wake	woke	woke/woken
lead	led	led	wear	wore	worn
lean	leant	leant	win	won	won
learn	learnt	learnt	write	wrote	written
leave	left	left			